GLASGOW

1   William of Orange (a bronze statue of 1735) looks towards the
medieval Cathedral

British Cities and Towns

GLASGOW

J. M. Reid

London
B. T. BATSFORD LTD

First Published 1956

PRINTED AND BOUND IN GREAT BRITAIN BY
WILLIAM CLOWES AND SONS, LIMITED, LONDON AND BECCLES
FOR THE PUBLISHERS
B. T. BATSFORD LIMITED
4, FITZHARDINGE STREET, PORTMAN SQUARE, LONDON, W.1

To
George Scott-Moncrieff
and
Russell Kirk
who suggested this book

PREFACE

THIS book has two aims: to tell the story of a great city whose past is not too well known either to the rest of the world or to some of its own people, and to suggest that Glasgow, to-day, is a place that is worth looking at.

The second of these aims may still seem the more surprising to Glasgow citizens themselves. Many of the details of Glasgow's history have been very thoroughly explored. I have tried to give a more generalised and simpler view.

The story is an unusual one. Glasgow is a community that has made itself. There is very little about its site that makes the development of a great city there seem an inevitable thing. Marxists might find difficulty in fixing on any material reason for its growth. It began as the seat of a bishopric which might, quite as easily, have been planted elsewhere. In Scotland only one of the other medieval sees has become a large modern town; and Aberdeen grew out of the old trading burgh rather than out of the little bishop's city that lay beside it. The rest of the old episcopal seats are either country towns or villages. To all appearance Glasgow might have been no bigger or more important but for the will and ingenuity of successive generations of Glasgow men.

Perhaps it is surprising that they should have thought so little of their town's good looks, at least in the last century, when most of Glasgow as we know it was being built. Perhaps they have been too busy to look about them. Perhaps they have so often heard it described as a grim, smoky, workaday place that they are afraid to compare it with more leisured cities, mellowed by time and generations of conscious good taste.

Certainly they have never thought of it as a *ville musée*. In a sense its architecture has been almost a folk art. To develop as it

9

did it must have been enjoyed, if only half consciously. Architects and builders themselves had, of course, as much knowledge and skill in the nineteenth century as they had in the Middle Ages, as the creators of Border ballads and peasant embroideries must have possessed in their day. But except when there was something surprisingly new or extravagant about it, their work was scarcely more discussed and criticised (except among professional colleagues) than the ballad-maker's is likely to have been. A little research is needed even to discover the names of the designers of many Glasgow buildings.

Yet the best, even the second-best, of them are worth preserving in our day, when nothing of the same sort can be expected to replace them. Our century is producing its own work, and the city, like other cities, will change. But we have a better chance than our grandfathers had to make the most of what the past has left us. Glasgow, which has heard some kindly words from learned visitors, is perhaps beginning to think that it may admire and care for its own fabric a little more thoroughly than it has done. I should like to believe that this book may encourage such a change of mind, though it is a daring thing for one who has no professional knowledge of architecture to preach on a subject of this sort.

It should be said that the series of buildings mentioned here is exemplary rather than exhaustive. Naturally I have given more attention to those that seem to me most obviously interesting and attractive. But there are scores of other Victorian and post-Victorian houses, churches, offices, and public buildings of one kind or another which deserve to be looked at. A thorough discussion of Glasgow architecture, its styles and designs, by a writer with a professional training behind him is very badly needed.

Summer, 1956 .. J. M. REID

CONTENTS

STREETS OF OLD GLASGOW

Provand's Lordship
GLASGOW CATHEDRAL
Barony Church
William II statue
Barony North Church
Wyndhead
Molendinar Burn
Bell the Brae
Site of Old College
Tolbooth Steeple
Glasgow Cross
Tron Steeple
Battle of the Butts
St. Andrew's Church
Site of Old Bridge

Kelvinside Academy
GREAT WESTERN
GR. WESTERN TERRACE
DOWANHILL
HILLHEAD
Pearce Lodge
PARTICK
University
Kelvingrove Park
River Kelvin
Museum & Art Galleries
Govan Church
GOVAN
Ibrox Stadium
PAISLEY ROAD WEST
GOVAN
POLLOKSHIELDS
TERREGLES
Crookston Castle
SCALE OF 1 MILE
0   ¼   ½   ¾   1
STRA
POLLOK
White Cart Water
Pollok House
Levern Water
BARRHEAD ROAD
POLLOKSHAWS

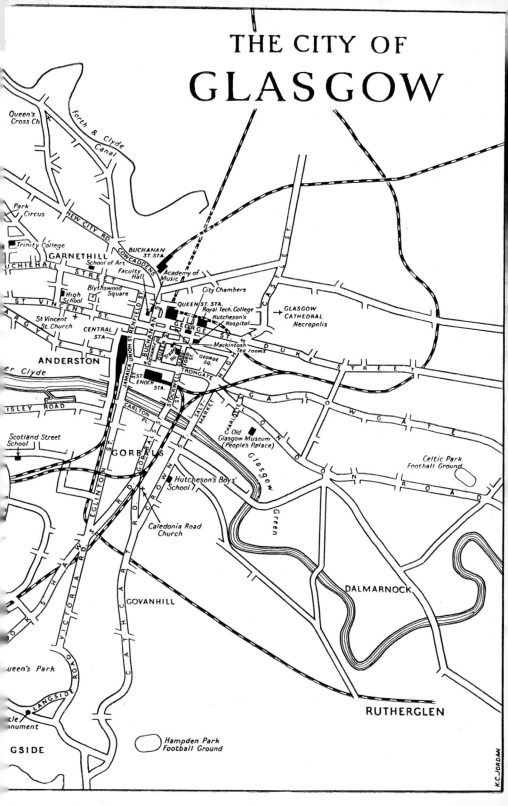

THE CITY OF
GLASGOW

Queen's
Cross Ch.

Forth & Clyde Canal

Park
Circus

Trinity College

GARNETHILL

School of Art

BUCHANAN
ST. STA.

Academy of
Music

UCHIEHALL STREET

Faculty
Hall

Blythswood
Square

City Chambers

High
School

ST. VINCENT
ST.

CENTRAL
STA.

St Vincent
St. Church

Queen ST. STA.
Royal Tech. College
Hutcheson's
Hospital

GLASGOW
CATHEDRAL
Necropolis

ANDERSTON

GEORGE
SQ.

Mackintosh
Tea rooms

DUKE STREET

er Clyde

JAMAICA UNION ST.

BUCHANAN

QUEEN ST.

ST.
ENOCH STA.

TRONGATE

STOCKWELL

HIGH ST.

GALLOWGATE

CARLTON PL.

SALT MARKET

CHARLOTTE ST.

LONDON ROAD

ISLEY ROAD

Scotland Street
School

GORBALS

Old
Glasgow Museum
(People's Palace)

Celtic Park
Football Ground

EGLINTON ST.

GORBALS

CROWN ST.

Hutcheson's Boys'
School

Glasgow Green

Caledonia Road
Church

DALMARNOCK

VICTORIA ROAD

CATHCART RD.

GOVANHILL

RUTHERGLEN

uEEN's Park

LANGSIDE ROAD

GSIDE

Hampden Park
Football Ground

K.C.JORDAN

ACKNOWLEDGMENT

THE Author and the Publishers are grateful to the following for supplying illustrations and for their permission to reproduce them in this book: Mr. George B. Alden and the *Scottish Field*, for figs. 22, 30, 39, 41, 42, and 43; Messrs. T. and R. Annan and Sons, for figs. 6, 9, 10, 16, 17, 23, 36, and 37; Mr. J. Allan Cash, F.I.B.P., F.R.P.S., for figs. 40 and 50; Glasgow Corporation, for the following from the Photographic Survey of Glasgow, 1954—Mr. D. Carmichael (Glasgow South Co-op Camera Club), for fig. 32; Mr. Andrew Gibb (Partick Camera Club), for fig. 52; Mr. F. Hooper (Partick Camera Club), for figs. 35 and 44; Miss A. M. Hanlon (Scottish Ramblers Federation Photographic Society), for fig. 34; Mr. D. H. Johnston (Drysdale Photographic Art Club), for fig. 26; Mr. John Logan (Scottish Ramblers Federation Photographic Society), for fig, 1; Mr. H. MacDonald (Scottish Ramblers Federation Photographic Society), for fig. 31; Mr. Charles Ritchie (Rolls Royce Camera Club), for fig. 5; Mr. John Robb (Glasgow South Co-op Camera Club), for fig. 51; Mr. R. B. Simpson (Knightswood Camera Club), for fig. 33. Mr. Donald B. MacCulloch, for figs. 15, 27, and 38; the National Trust for Scotland and the Ministry of Works for fig. 13; the Old Glasgow Museum, for fig. 11; Messrs. George Outram and Co. Ltd., for figs. 3, 14, and 19; Mr. Paul Shillabeer, F.R.P.S., for figs. 2 and 4; Mr. W. Suschitzsky, for figs. 45, 46, and 49. The quotation from William Bolitho in Chapter IX is reproduced by permission of Messrs. Putnam and Co. Ltd.

The author's thanks are due to those who have given him help and advice, though none of them must be blamed for the possibly eccentric views expressed in this book. He must mention particularly Mr. Alexander Wright, F.R.I.B.A., Mr. Alfred G. Lochhead, A.R.I.B.A., Mr. H. Jefferson Barnes, Sir John Spencer Muirhead, D.S.O., LL.D., Mr. John Dunlop, of Baillie's Institute, Mr. George Emslie, Mitchell Library, and, for help with illustrations, Dr Stewart Henderson, Director of the Glasgow Museums and Art Galleries, Mr. Adam Stevens of the Glasgow Photographic Survey, Miss Elspeth Gallie of the Old Glasgow Museum (now Mrs. William Buchanan), Mr. Sydney Harrison and Mr. A. M. Burnie. His daughter Jean has struggled successfully and encouragingly with his handwriting.

14

LIST OF ILLUSTRATIONS

15

CHAPTER ONE

The Legend

NOT Glasgow, Mont., or Glasgow, Ky., but Glasgow, Scotland. Outside the Mississippi Basin, the warning may scarcely seem necessary. Yet considering its past and present Glasgow, Scotland, is rather oddly shrouded from the world's consciousness.

Though many hundreds of thousands (perhaps millions) of Scotsmen, Irishmen, Englishmen, Poles, Ukrainians, and Balts have passed through Glasgow to the new countries beyond the Atlantic, though Glasgow-built ships have entered every harbour in the world and Glasgow-made machines are in every continent the name is not so noticeably scattered over the map as the names of some smaller Scots towns. Though it has been the largest city in Scotland for a century and a half past—as overwhelmingly large, comparatively speaking, as London is in England—it is not too well known even to its neighbours in this island. Edinburgh people, who live only forty miles away, have been heard to speak of a journey through Glasgow in the tone that might be used to describe a successful crossing of the Sahara. And when, in 1950, Glasgow University invited the world's chief seats of learning to send representatives to the celebration of its five-hundredth birthday, some surprise seems to have been felt in other parts of Britain that an industrial town, a sort of Scottish Halifax or Wolverhampton, could have centuries of academic history behind it.

Yet Glasgow was an ancient place, as Scottish cities go, before its university was thought of; and the observant tourist who comes to it expecting something like the Five Towns of Staffordshire or a Lancashire county borough will surely find himself surprised.

Where Glasgow lies the river Clyde has just met the tide some 90 miles from its source in the green Lanarkshire hills, and is flowing north-westward to the sea. When the first fisher-people put their dug-out canoes into the river, they settled beside burns that ran down to the north bank between a series of steep, gravelly, little ridges, from which one could look north again towards a range of greater heights, the Campsies and the Kilpatricks. Facing these heights, Agricola, the first invading Roman general to reach this part of the world, built his line of forts. Half a century later they became the turf wall that ran across the narrow neck of lowland between the Firth of Clyde (which belongs to the Atlantic) and the Firth of Forth (which is the North Sea).

The Romans' hold on southern Scotland was brief and much interrupted, but it had some lasting effects. The position of Glasgow may be one of them. The town grew up where a Roman road leading towards the wall cut across the little glen in which the Mellindonor* Burn ran to its meeting with the Clyde less than a mile away. Beside the Mellindonor's mouth a ford led across the river to what must have been the natural route south-westwards towards the Ayrshire coast. It seems possible that Glasgow owes its existence to the crossing of these two roads, where, in the Middle Ages, the line of the High Street met the line of the Drygate and the Rottenrow. But there were many other fords on the Clyde besides the one which became the site of the old Glasgow Bridge, most of them leading to some sort of crossroad. Legend is not always wrong, even when it seems most improbable. And legend says that Glasgow grew where it did because two bulls stopped there with the cart they had been pulling.

On the cart was the body of an aged Christian, Fergus. And behind it walked a young priest, Mungo, the grandson of kings, whose name is the first in Glasgow's story.

Everything in the city's rather complicated coat of arms commemorates the saint. A century or two back, Protestant children

---

* Elsewhere in this book the later spelling "Molendinar", is used. This is apparently a Latinisation. There were medieval mills on its stream.

made a sort of nursery rhyme about them, unnecessarily sceptical but evocative:

> Yon's the tree that never grew,
> Yon's the bird that never flew,
> Yon's the fish that never swam,
> Yon's the bell that never rang.

They were wrong about the square handbell, at any rate. This typical relic of a Celtic saint was still in existence more than a thousand years after his coming—which was presumably about the year 540. The rest of the armorial objects belong to St. Mungo's legend, which, we are assured, lived not only in books but in the "streets and lanes of the city" about the beginning of the thirteenth century.

Loth or Leudonus, the half-pagan king of Lothian, had a daughter, Thenew, who was beautiful, innocent, and a Christian. She was wooed by a royal youth, Ewen, the son of Urien, but was determined to remain a virgin. The beardless Ewen, disguised as a girl, overcame her without her knowledge. When she was found to be with child her father ordered her to be thrown down from the top of Traprain Law, the site of an ancient hill town (presumably his tribal capital) which the East Lothian County Council is now quarrying away for road metal. The princess was saved by a miracle. She was then carried to the coast of the Firth of Forth, a few miles away, and sent to sea alone in a coracle which brought her to the opposite coast at Culross. There, on the shore, her son was born. Mother and child were cared for by St. Serf, who had his monastery close by, and who called the child Munghu, which means "dear one" and Cyndeyrn or Kentigern, which means "chief lord".*

Mungo became the saint's favourite pupil. He was not only learned and virtuous beyond other boys of the saint's school: he also showed miraculous powers. He was able to draw fire from a frozen branch (in the hands of the heraldic painters this became

---

* Kentigern, which became the accepted, one may say the official, name of the saint in later records, is Gaelic. Munghu or Mungo and Cyndeyrn are British or Welsh. It seems most unlikely that a Gaelic name can have been known among the British Lowlanders of the sixth century. Mungo has, in fact, remained the more popular of the two names and has been passed on to many generations of Scots boys.

"the tree that never grew") and to restore St. Serf's pet robin to life after the unruly pupils had killed it—this was "the bird that never flew". When he reached manhood he left Culross to spread religion in places where the teaching of the early missionaries had been lost. Just beyond the Forth, at Carnock, near Stirling, he found the holy man, Fergus, on his death-bed. Fergus asked that, when he died, his body should be placed on a cart drawn by two untamed bulls and that where they stopped it should be buried.

This was done. The bulls travelled thirty miles or so across the hills to a point on the Mellindonor, just north of the line of the Roman road. There was an old Christian cemetery on the edge of the glen there, blessed by St. Ninian more than a century earlier. The place, it is said, was called Cathures—perhaps it was the fort of some local chieftain. It was to be re-named Cleschu or Glaschu, which, according to the oldest etymology, means "dear community" (cara familia), Mungo's description of the monastery he founded there.* The saint made his home beside Fergus's burial place and was soon chosen bishop by the king and the Christian clergy and people of the district, "albeit they were few in number".

A pagan reaction drove him out, and he took refuge in Wales, where he is said to have founded the monastery which became the village-city of St. Asaph, named after one of Mungo's disciples. He was recalled to the north, however, by a victorious champion of Christianity, King Rederech, who was his friend and supporter to the end of his long life. St. Mungo settled first at Hoddam, in Dumfriesshire, which remained an ecclesiastical centre long after his day, and then returned to Glasgow.

The saint showed a remarkable interest in the King's domestic happiness. The Queen, Languoreth, became passionately interested in a handsome young warrior. She was rash enough to give him a ring which had been a gift from her husband. King Rederech suspected the worst, not unjustly. When he and his rival were

---

* There are many other suggested explanations of the name Glasgow—"Dear stream", "dear green place", "green hollows" even "Greyhound"—an alleged nickname for St. Mungo.

resting on the banks of the Clyde on a hunting expedition he snatched the ring from the sleeping warrior's hand, threw it into the river, and, going home, angrily demanded that his wife should show him the precious thing.

The lover fled. The Queen was in danger. But she appealed to St. Mungo, who told her messenger to cast a line into the Clyde, which at once brought out "the fish that never swam", a fine salmon with the lost ring in its belly. Queen Languoreth was able to show her jewel again before the court, and lasting peace returned to the royal household.

Mungo and Rederech ruled together over a happy and increasingly pious people. The saint and his monks made a series of missionary journeys not only through Rederech's kingdom but also, it seems, among the Picts of the north-east. The great Irish apostle of the Picts, St. Columba of Iona, was already working there. Rederech certainly knew him, and perhaps this contact brought about the visit of Columba to Glasgow which has a prominent place in Mungo's official biography. Mungo died and was buried beside the altar of his church above the Mellindonor, perhaps in the year 603. A few months later his royal friend was laid beside him and 665 saints of the monastery were soon to share their resting place in the ground where Glasgow Cathedral now stands.

Perhaps all this has the air of fantasy. It is hard for us to believe in the revivified robin, in the miracle of the salmon, in the wolf and stag which St. Mungo is said to have yoked together when no other beasts could be found to draw a plough. The best authorities say that St. Serf, Mungo's teacher, probably lived about a century after King Rederech's time.

But Rederech himself certainly belongs to history. He was Rhydderch Hael, who "reigned in the Rock of Clyde" (which is Dumbarton) and was the founder of a British Kingdom, later called Strathclyde, that stretched from Loch Lomond to the Derwent, in Cumberland, and lasted, in one form or another, for six centuries. Ewen (or Owen) and his father Urien, King of Rheged, are historic figures too, leaders of the British resistance to the invading Angles in Northumberland. There are a whole series of points in St. Mungo's story which seem to give a lively and probable picture of life just beyond the borders of the Roman Empire in the obscure years when the Roman power had collapsed in the west and Christianity was gradually establishing itself in the Celtic countries. The new, the enthusiastic, half-instructed child who longed to be a second Virgin Mother, is the sort of figure whom that age must sometimes have known. The struggle between half-pagan, half-Christianised Britons who had to meet the attacks of wholly pagan rivals, Celts or Teutons, is more convincingly described in legends like St. Mungo's than in any of the scanty chronicles.

We can see the first Glasgow as Mungo left it, a collection of little huts and oratories for his monks looking down on the Roman road, long deserted by the legionaries, but still used by the travellers to and from the west. It would be sheltered by an earthen rampart, and beside it there may have been a fort for the king's use—though he had another dwelling at Partick, three miles away in the modern city. The forest crept close to this little settlement, but the spreading fields were perhaps pushing it back, and Glasgow was already a name for religion and learning as far away as the hills of Cumberland.

There is a hint of something besides history and hagiography in St. Mungo's story. It is linked with the great new romantic literature which was growing up in western Europe when the saint's life was written by the monk Jocelin of Furness at the end of the twelfth century. Jocelin does not mention King Arthur, and Mungo's name does not occur in any Arthurian story, though there is a trace of it in Welsh records and verse. But, according to the reckoning of the romance writers he should have been Arthur's grand-nephew twice over, for in the romances his mother's father becomes Lot, King of Lothian and Orkney, the husband of Margaause, Arthur's sister, and the father of Gawain and Gareth. The historic Urien Rheged becomes Uriens, King of Gore, husband of another and more famous (or infamous) sister, Morgane le Fay. And Mungo's father, Ewen, is Yvain li Aoutres, the Knight with the Lion, who fought for the Lady of the Fountain in the enchanted forest of Broceliande.

This is certainly a surprising background, or shadow of a background for a city which helped to launch the Industrial Age. Yet it is not so inappropriate as it might seem. Modern Glasgow has always prided itself on being a particularly hard-headed, practical place, but Glasgow men have often been inclined to take a romantic view of their city and their world. There has been at least the hint of a romantic spirit in their art, in their ambitions, even in their failures, something that goes naturally with the soft light, the mists, the changing, glowing colours of the western scene. If a faint mist of romance hangs about Glasgow's origins this is, perhaps, very much as it should be.

CHAPTER TWO

The Bishops' City

603 to 1560

PROBABLY there would have been no Glasgow but for St. Mungo: no city, at any rate, for there were plenty of other sites on the Clyde better suited, one would think, to foster a great town. In St. Mungo's day, and for centuries after it, indeed, Glasgow was no more than a village. But the little place and its church remained a centre of religion in the west country. And when the great organiser of medieval Scotland, the prince who was to be King David I, began his work, Glasgow was the first of the bishoprics that he set out to establish, or re-establish, on the regular Roman pattern of his time.

In a sense, David was the latest successor of Mungo's King Rhydderch—he was Prince, or Earl, of Cumbria, the country of the Cymry, the Welsh country, which stretched from Loch Lomond to the Solway. But the people of Cumbria no longer spoke Welsh.

Five hundred years had passed since St. Mungo's day, and when an attempt was made to trace the possessions of his church, the enquirers seem to have come to the conclusion that the race he preached to had vanished altogether, driven into exile and replaced by heathen tribes of various nations. Certainly this was not so. There is no reason to think that the basic population of the west of Scotland has ever changed radically in historic times. But the people had been beaten about by wars and invasions. By David's day most of them talked Gaelic, just as, a few generations later, the descendants would be speaking English (or Scots).

The British kingdom of Strathclyde had been the least fortunate of the little states which were finally fused into Scotland.

2   Glasgow Cathedral: the Nave looking East to the Choir

3 The East End and
Chapter House

4 The Lower Church:
St. Mungo's Tomb

THE CATHEDRAL

For a while a large part of it was overrun by the Northumbrian Angles. Later it was partitioned between the Angles and the Picts. When it regained its independence it was harassed (like many other parts of Britain) by Viking invaders. Perhaps the oldest carved work in modern Glasgow shows some Scandinavian influence—the remarkable sarcophagus and grave stones from the Church of Govan, which is said to have been founded by a contemporary of Mungo's, St. Constantine, a Cornish king who had become a missionary. Finally Strathclyde (or Cumbria) was converted into a sort of apanage for the heirs of the growing Scottish kingdom. Probably the first of them to rule St. Mungo's country in this way was David's grandfather, the "gentle Duncan" who was killed by Macbeth. David's son was the last. But David himself was the prince who left his mark on Glasgow, and Scotland.

His business was the modernising and Europeanising of a country that lay on the outskirts of feudal Christendom. And modernisation, in his day, meant the bringing in of feudal lords, the establishment of bishoprics, abbeys and towns, the organising of laws and law courts. He settled French-speaking knights in masterless lands—they were the best possible safeguard against the sort of Anglo-Norman conquest which began the desolation of Ireland just after his day. The most important of these from Glasgow's point of view (and, finally, from Scotland's) was his steward, Walter, whom he established in Renfrewshire, and who became the ancestor of the Stewart kings, and of all other Stewarts and Stuarts.

One of David's first objects was to reorganise the Church in what was left of the old Kingdom of Strathclyde. No doubt there had been bishops in Glasgow and Strathclyde since Mungo's time, though the one name about which we can feel fairly certain is that of Sedulius (probably a Scot) in the eighth century. There are faint traces of a struggle between the prince and the Archbishop of York over the choice and consecration of a new bishop: for a century and more the English Primates (of York and Canterbury) tried to control the Scottish Church. About the year 1110, however, David's former tutor, John Achaius (no doubt a Gael whose original name was Eochaidh) was consecrated Bishop of Glasgow by the Pope. The first stone cathedral was built over St. Mungo's tomb and consecrated in 1136. Important lands, including most of those on which the great modern city now stands, and a part of what is now north Lanarkshire, were given or restored to St. Mungo's church.

The first bishops are rather dim figures, though some of them (John Achaius included) were active in the affairs of the Scottish kingdom. We have one startling glimpse of Glasgow in this medieval dawn—of a prelate returning thanks to St. Mungo as he held in his hands the head of an invader, Somerled, who had been called king in Argyll and the Isles. There was no organised town beside the cathedral of Bishop Herbert's day—a little church, shaded by a grove of trees that surrounded the tomb where Mungo had laid Fergus—though there was a settlement, old enough, no doubt, in whose "streets and lanes" St. Mungo's biographer could claim to have picked up traditions of the saint's life. There could be no city till a bishop was ready to establish one. The King could found burghs on his own lands: two had been set up beside royal castles near Glasgow—at Rutherglen and Renfrew. But the castle and burgh of Glasgow had to belong to its lord. It was the great Bishop Jocelin who seriously set about making a city for himself.

Jocelin had been Abbot of Melrose, one of King David's foundations. He was consecrated by the Primate of Denmark, in order to defeat the claim of York to supremacy over the Scottish Church. He was a diplomatist at a time when Scottish diplomacy was active and very badly needed.

About the time of Jocelin's election as bishop, both the King and the kingdom lost their freedom. Young William, called the Lion, was taken prisoner when he was trying to recapture lost lands in the north of England. He was forced to swear allegiance to his formidable cousin, Henry II, as overlord of Scotland. At this unpromising moment, the new Bishop of Glasgow insisted that the Scottish Church was subject to no one but the Pope. He spoke in Rome for the King as well as for the clergy. Finally, in 1188, he won a decision that the Scottish bishops were directly dependent on the Holy See—a year before King William bought back his country's independence from Richard Cœur-de-Lion.

Bishop Jocelin was as active for his diocese as for his King. He rebuilt his cathedral, though only a fragment of his work remains in the present church. And, about the year 1176, he obtained a charter from King William allowing him to establish a burgh in Glasgow with all the privileges which the King's burghs possessed. A few years later, this grant was solemnly confirmed by Pope Alexander III who took the city under his protection.

Glasgow, then, was a new town at the end of the twelfth century. But with Bishop Jocelin's foundation the place began to take a form which was fixed for six hundred years, and is still recognisable, though only two buildings of the Middle Ages can now be seen.

It was the form of a cross, twice repeated. At the top of the town (still the Townhead) were the cathedral and the bishop's castle, standing just above the glen of the Molendinar. The houses to the south of them belonged chiefly to the clergy—before the end of the Middle Ages there were thirty-two canons of the cathedral chapter, most of whom had manses or lodgings. Clergy houses surrounded the upper cross, the Wyndhead, where the streets that followed the line of the Roman road met the Kirkgait, now Cathedral Street. South from this, the Hiegait (High Street) sloped to the centre of the merchant town, which is still Glasgow Cross. The street running east from this is the Gallowgate, for it led to the site of the town gallows. Continuing its line westward from the cross was St. Thenew's Gait (now the Trongate) which reached towards a chapel dedicated to St. Mungo's mother, whose name, oddly corrupted by time, remains in St. Enoch's Square. The north to south line ran down from the Cross in the Walkergait—the street of the fullers—which is now the Saltmarket, This ended where it met the Molendinar, curving west to join the Clyde. When a bridge was built beside the burn's mouth in the thirteenth century, the Briggait (Bridgegate) joined it to the Walkergait, and another short street, the Fishergait (now Stockwell) ran up from the bridge-head to meet St. Thenew's Gait.

All of this was not in Bishop Jocelin's day (or for long after) a closely built town. It is possible that when he began to lay it out, the ground was clearer of houses than it had once been: most of Glasgow may have been burnt during Somerled's invasion. In the new foundation strips of land ran out from the streets. A house would normally be built on the street front: behind it was a garden and perhaps an orchard. A few of the houses were stone-built and even fortified: little castles or peels. Others were of wood or wattle. But, from the beginning, there must have been a good many substantial buildings, since a number of plots were given to great monasteries, like Paisley Abbey, or to powerful bodies, like the Knights Templar. Glasgow never had fortified town walls on the grander medieval scale, but there was a wall of a kind, linking the garden dykes at the back of the "closes" and there were gates where the streets met the open country.

This early Glasgow was a green place, set among green forests and parti-coloured moorland. Though, from its earliest days as a city most of its people were no doubt clergy, small merchants, fishermen, woodworkers and craftsmen, most of its lay burgesses were, in effect, free peasants too. They fed themselves from their own land. Between, and beyond, the houses and gardens on the lines of the streets there were "crofts"—fields in which each citizen had his share. And beyond these again, fringing the river and running out to the east and north were the common lands where beasts were pastured, peats and wood were cut for fuel, and stone was quarried for building. As the town spread, parts of these were broken for ploughing, but till the eighteenth century the town's herdsmen still drove the householders' cattle to pasture and brought them home for the milking. The herdsmen were, like other officials, elected yearly at the head courts, where the burgesses, actual owners of town houses and land, met under the sky, at Easter or Whitsunday on the Symmer-hill (on the slopes above the modern New City Road) and at Michaelmas and Yule near the river—until long experience of the weather and the progress of building induced them to gather in the Tolbooth or Town's House at the Cross.

To begin with, much of the town's business seems to have been done at these meetings, where every burgess could speak. The magistrates were probably nominated there—or at least the candidates for the magistracy, for the final choice was made by the bishop, as lord of the city. Burgesses everywhere had what amounted to a monopoly of internal trade—not only in their town itself but in the district round it—except at public fairs. In Glasgow's case the bishop's lands were dependent on the burgh traders in this way. The men of royal burghs also had special rights of trading outside their own bounds and assured protection from the king in doing so: and, though Glasgow did not have the name of a royal burgh until the seventeenth century, it seems fairly clear that its merchants enjoyed most of these privileges from the beginning. They held their great Fair in the second week of July. The original date for its beginning, July 7th, apparently commemorates the dedication of the cathedral. Very early this became a time for the settling of accounts throughout the west of Scotland. Later other fairs were added. They had their markets weekly on Thursdays.

Though the earliest relics of the place are boats (of a sort), and though it now builds ships for a large part of the world, Glasgow was not a sea-port in the Middle Ages. It had rich salmon fisheries. It became, before long, one of the main centres of the trade in salt herring. But, for commerce, the River Clyde was no better than a shallow canal which probably silted and grew shallower still as the centuries passed. Even the tiny sea-going ships of those times could scarcely get beyond Dumbarton, sixteen miles away, or, at best, Renfrew, ten miles nearer. Foreign goods had to be transferred into lighters before they could be brought into Glasgow. The burgh flourished and grew partly as a market for the West Highlands, but mainly on the wealth of the Church and its own fertile lands. All the south-west of Scotland, except Galloway, was subject to its bishop, and in the century after Jocelin's day a new energy ran through the whole country.

Through the whole of Scotland, indeed, one may say, through

the whole of Christendom. The thirteenth century was the crown of the Middle Ages, before divisions in the Church, imperialist adventures like the Hundred Years War, new barbarian invasions, long and savage dynastic struggles, the disaster of the Black Death, had begun to tear the heart out of that feudal society. Over most of western Europe great new buildings were springing up, the structure of government was growing firmer (yet more liberal), there was a new civility among the peoples: and notably in Scotland. The king's peace spread over the country: after the defeat of the last Norwegian invasion in 1263 there were no serious foreign wars. New churches and castles and spreading fields were everywhere. Out of this age of hope and progress came the new cathedral of Glasgow.

It was begun, most probably, quite early in the thirteenth century, but the man most concerned with it was William de Bondington, who was Chancellor of Scotland when he was elected bishop in 1232. It is the one great church of the Scottish mainland that has survived since the Middle Ages with very little change or damage to its fabric: even before the ruin of so many cathedrals and abbeys Scotland can scarcely have seen a church interior more impressive in the purity of its design.

The exterior must, in its day, have been nearly as striking, with its great central spire, rising to 220 feet, and the cliff-like bulk of its square east end. These things, indeed, remain. But one must first meet the west end of the church and here Victorian ideas of "improvement" have done far more damage than time, war, or Reformers. The western façade was once flanked by a tower on one side and a tall, buttressed, fifteenth-century consistory house on the other. In the name of Gothic "correctness" these were removed in 1846–8. Prints and paintings show that they had a most characteristically Scottish air about them. To-day the west front, its great window coarsened by Victorian hands, has a rather mean and barnlike look, most unworthy of what lies behind it.

The church is entirely Gothic and almost entirely in the First Pointed style. The site was fixed by St. Mungo's tomb, which lies on the slope of the Molendinar Glen, just below the hill top where the bishop's castle stood and the town of Glasgow ended. To give it a properly commanding position, the church, too, must seem to stand on the hill ridge. The nave rests on the level, but to carry the choir, with the high altar over the saint's grave, it was necessary to build in two storeys. For that reason we have the very remarkable Lower Church (not strictly a crypt, since nearly all of it is above ground level) whose great pillars and walls support the choir above them. Here is the square stone platform that marks St. Mungo's tomb.

The Lower Church is reached by stairways from the crossing, where the soaring nave meets the shallow, scarcely visible transepts and the steps of the choir. A massive stone screen of the late fifteenth century stands above the steps. The choir is to-day the Reformed High Kirk of Glasgow. Its pews and its modern, often interesting, stained glass apart, however, it is in most respects as its builders left it, full of strength and light.

The latest part of the church is, perhaps, the one that seems to take us closest to the beginnings of Glasgow. As you step down from the crossing into what was evidently meant to be the sub-structure of an extended south transept, you find yourself facing a rather primitive-looking carving which shows a figure lying between the high wheels of a cart. Round it are the words: "This is ye Ile of Car Fergus". This undercroft was not built before the end of the fifteenth century, but it is supposed to cover part of the cemetery consecrated by St. Ninian a thousand years earlier, and the site of Fergus's grave. The little place now shines with colour since its elaborate bosses have been repainted in the medieval style.

In the Lower Church, the faces of Bishop Bondington and of two kings who saw the building of his church, Alexander II and Alexander III, look down on us from the bosses of the vaulting. And a headless figure in the dimness of the eastern chapels commemorates the Bishop of Glasgow who made the deepest mark in history.

He was Robert Wishart, who had held the see for thirteen years or more through the time of peace and prosperity before King Alexander III fell to his death from a cliff path in 1286.

He was chosen one of the six Guardians of the Kingdom for the infant princess of Norway who was Alexander's heiress. Very soon he, with the other Guardians, had to meet the efforts of Edward I of England, the conqueror of the Welsh to win control of Scotland too.

King Edward's ambitions were formidable. The populations he controlled were perhaps ten, perhaps nearer twenty, times greater than Scotland's. He was a far-sighted ruler and a resourceful soldier. He was also an able propagandist with the capacity (so valuable to politicians in our own time) for believing his own propaganda on suitable occasions. His subjects and neighbours seldom found it possible to trust the King of England's promises for very long. Yet he boasted the motto "Keep Troth" (*Pactum Serva*) and seems to have been sincerely shocked when other people broke the oaths he had extorted from them, as most of the Scots leaders did time after time.

At this point we reach an important turn in European, even in world history: the plain appearance of a genuine national patriotism affecting all classes in a kingdom. Here medieval Scotland produced something that Christendom had never seen before, and it would scarcely be too much to claim that nationalism of this sort began in or near Glasgow. Its leaders were William Wallace, the son of a local knight; Robert Bruce, Earl of Carrick, a west-country noble, and Bishop Wishart. In a sense it is paradoxical that churchmen, belonging to the most obviously supranational of all medieval institutions, should have come out so strongly on the side of the Scottish nation: yet this is not so surprising when one looks back on the long struggle of the Glasgow bishops—and those of other Scots sees—to maintain their independence against authorities in England. When, after the little queen's death, Wishart denounced King Edward's claim to superiority over Scotland as something new and unheard of he was repeating, in another form, what Bishop Jocelin had said more than a century earlier.

Some years later, Pope Boniface VIII, usually a friend to Scotland, accused the Bishop of Glasgow of having been "the first promoter" of the struggle between the Scottish nation and

King Edward. This was certainly an exaggeration: Edward I himself was at the root of the quarrel. But undoubtedly there was something to exaggerate. Wishart seems to have been one of the chief organisers of the first rising against the English after their conquest of the country. He was imprisoned. He made his peace and then rebelled again.

Glasgow itself probably* saw its first battle while its bishop was a prisoner or a fugitive. His castle (where the Royal Infirmary now stands, beside the cathedral) was garrisoned by an English force under Anthony Bek, the warlike Bishop of Durham. William Wallace, at the beginning of his year of victories, moved on the city from Ayr. With half his little force he seized the wooden bridge across the Clyde and pushed into the town. The rest of his men were with his uncle, the laird of Auchinleck (no doubt an ancestor of James Boswell), who had agreed to "bear up the Bishop of Durham's tail"—that is, to take the English in the rear. The garrison moved out of the castle to meet Wallace in the High Street. Then Auchinleck broke in over the Molendinar and up the Drygate, on the line of the Roman road. The battle was fought out at the Bell o' the Brae, the steep slope of street just south of the upper cross. Bek and his surviving men were forced to break away into the woods—no doubt in the general direction of modern Duke Street. They took refuge in Bothwell Castle, the chief fortress of middle Clydesdale, which was afterwards besieged and taken by the Scots.

Glasgow had to suffer for its bishop's defiance. King Edward himself occupied the town in 1301. Thrice he made offerings to St. Mungo, but his Irish foot soldiers dealt so hardly with the place and the bishop's lands round it that taxes could not be raised, even by English collectors, a year later.

Now the long war had reached a crisis: an end, as King Edward no doubt hoped. The forces on the Scots side were worn down. France was ceasing to support them. The leaders, who had kept a kind of Resistance Government going, could not maintain themselves. Bishop Wishart surrendered and had his

* The story of this fight comes from Blind Harry's epic, but it probably has tradition behind it.

lands restored in 1304. A year later Wallace was betrayed to his pursuers at Robroyston near Glasgow—the place is now part of the city. He was carried to London and hanged, drawn, and quartered at Smithfield, insisting that he had never been a traitor to England, since he had never accepted Edward as his king. Within eight months, a new King of Scots, Robert Bruce, was in Glasgow.

He was a man with a load of misfortune, excommunicate, penniless, with no army behind him. The Bishop of Glasgow was now, by medieval standards, an old man, enjoying a sort of peace. Yet he rallied at once to this forlorn hope: it seems likely enough, indeed, that he advised Bruce to make himself King. In defiance, it would seem, of the Church's law, he absolved him of the crime which appeared to make his adventure most desperate. Among the cathedral vestments he found robes and a royal banner that could be used for a coronation at Scone, which still seemed the proper sacring place of Scottish kings, though King Edward had carried off the holy stone on which each new King of Scots had been seated. King Robert was crowned, pursued, defeated. And when the castle of Cupar, in Fife, fell to the English, the Bishop of Glasgow was captured there, in armour.

King Edward was almost as pleased as if Bruce himself had been made prisoner. But because he was a churchman, Wishart could not be executed like King Robert's brothers, who were taken about the same time. The Pope would not depose him. But he spent eight years in English prisons. It was not till after the King's decisive victory at Bannockburn that he was freed in an exchange of prisoners. He came home, blind and aged, to a city that was now at peace, though the lands of the bishopric had been given, for a time, to the man who betrayed Wallace, Sir John Menteith. Two years after his liberation he was dead.

The Bishop's patriotism had fruits which were perhaps even more important for Glasgow than for his country. In a Scotland subdued like Ireland or Wales Glasgow would probably have become a northern Tuam or St. Asaph. On the whole, the fourteenth century was not a prosperous age for Scotland. The victorious peace was followed by new invasions

36

from the south. For long years on end there was no effective king; then a new dynasty had to establish itself against difficulties. But through most of this turmoil Glasgow prospered. The diocese had been the second in wealth and size, but St. Andrews, the senior bishopric, had been far more important. The new kings, however, had a strong interest in the west country. Robert Bruce, who owed so much to Wishart, spent a good part of his last years of pain and glory at Cardross on the Clyde. His grandson, Robert the High Steward, who became the leader of the national forces and, in the end, the first Stewart king, had been the most powerful lord in the neighbourhood of Glasgow.

It may have been Stewart influence which gave Glasgow its first and only cardinal. The name of this prince of the Church, Bishop Walter Wardlaw, is not otherwise very distinguished. But wealth and privileges continued to flow towards Glasgow in a gentle but fairly steady stream. The most magnificent of the bishops, John Cameron, was secretary to James I and chancellor of the kingdom. The tall sacristy of the cathedral is his work: its central pillar bears his arms and his king's. Royal influence no doubt helped his successor, Bishop William Turnbull, to establish the second Scottish university in Glasgow. King James II, who backed it, held a canon's stall in the cathedral.

James IV, his grandson and the most brilliant of the Stewart kings, was also an honorary canon, and it was in his reign that the see of Glasgow reached the height of its glory. Throughout the centuries of her struggle against the claims of the English archbishops, Scotland had had no archbishopric of her own, and when, in 1472, the Pope gave this dignity to St. Andrews, the other bishops were rebellious and the laity by no means enthusiastic. Having reconciled themselves to the existence of one archbishop, however, the King and his Parliament saw no reason why Scotland should not have two. England had York as well as Canterbury, and in a letter to the Pope, the Scots Parliament asked that Glasgow should be made the York of Scotland. It was a typical gesture of national self-assurance—had not Scotland just equipped itself with two universities, to match Oxford and Cambridge?

No doubt the personality of the first Archbishop had something to do with Glasgow's promotion. Robert Blacader was a valued servant of the crown as well as "ane noble, wyse and godlie man". He was a diplomat, much concerned in the long and complicated negotiations for the marriage of King James, whose alliance was sought after in many courts. The Catholic Kings of Spain tried to bribe the Archbishop with a cardinal's hat. In the end, however, he negotiated the most important wedding settlement in British history. The treaty which, in the end, united the Scots and English thrones was ratified in 1502 at the High Altar of Glasgow Cathedral. Next year—just a century before their great-grandson, James VI became James I of England—the Archbishop married his King to Margaret Tudor, the daughter of Henry VII. Blacader died five years later on a pilgrimage to Jerusalem, which was also a diplomatic mission to Venice. It was he who made the last important additions to Glasgow Cathedral—the Fergus Aisle and the great choir screen.

Glasgow was certainly a modest York. Yet, on the face of things, it was far better fitted to be an ecclesiastical capital than to grow into a great industrial city. As a port it was far inferior to York itself. Its gateway to the ocean (its predestined Hull, one might have thought) was Irvine on the Ayrshire coast, thirty miles away. Its Sheffield, on the coal and iron fields, might have been Hamilton or Airdrie. The central point in the next three centuries of Glasgow's story is really the series of decisions or accidents by which the Scottish York was changed into something quite different, the teeming centre of a nation's trade and industry.

Meanwhile, Glasgow was becoming an increasingly pleasant and prosperous place. The one house that has survived from medieval Glasgow dates from just before the first archbishop's time. It is a three-storeyed building with crow-stepped gables which looks across the square to the cathedral. Its name, Provand's Lordship, tells something of its history, for part of the house was the manse of the prebendary of Barlanark, the only member of the cathedral chapter whose revenues came from an estate and not from the endowments of a neighbouring parish.

His canonry lands were (and still are) called Provan from the Latin *prebenda*. Provand's Lordship is now a museum with a collection of old prints and furnishings. The oldest part of the building, however, was intended to house the clergy of St. Nicholas's Hospital, which stood close by. The hospital, an alms-house for twelve poor men, was one proof that Glasgow was becoming a better provided, more comfortable town. Arch-bishop Blacader's nephew was soon to found another near by, "for the poor and indigent casually coming thereto", perhaps as pilgrims to St. Mungo's shrine. There had been a leper hospital just beyond the bridge and south of the city for several centuries.

  Glasgow itself did not make an impression of poverty or indigence. In the mid-fifteenth century, an English agent found it "a goodly cytee, where plentiful is the countree also", with abundance of corn and cattle. He suggested, in fact, that Glasgow would be the best place for the convergence of three conquering English armies, who would be well fed when they got there! Spies are notoriously apt to find information that is likely to please their employers. But Glasgow was certainly growing in size and prosperity more rapidly than most Scottish towns. Judging by its contributions to national revenue, it was now the eighth or ninth burgh of Scotland and the richest of the strictly episcopal cities. Its craftsmen were organising themselves more tightly: the guilds which were so powerful in Continental towns of the early Middle Ages scarcely appear in Scotland before the fifteenth century. The first of them to obtain a clear recognition of its privileges in Glasgow, the Incorporation of Skinners, did not do so till 1516. The town administration had also taken a firmer shape. Since the city's foundation there had been magis-trates chosen by the bishop from a list of names submitted to him by leading burgesses who became the town council. To begin with, apparently, they were all called provosts (*prepositi*): later they were bailies,★ and a single provost, as president of the municipality and deputy of the bishop in his dealings with the burgesses, does not appear till 1453.

★ The equivalent English word is "bailiff", but the office is more like that of an English alderman.

He was a Stewart, the son of a knight from the Border country. In this we can see a shadow of troubles to come. When Glasgow was still no more than a sort of outgrowth of the cathedral its affairs were of interest only to churchmen, craftsmen, and small traders. But as it became, more and more, a sort of provincial capital, to which revenue flowed from most parts of the west, with powerful ecclesiastical courts, and growing trade, the great men of the neighbourhood began to feel that they ought to have more control over the place and its wealth. The archbishops remained powerful and respected figures until the Reformation. Unlike many Scottish bishoprics and abbeys during the last generation of the Roman Church's power, the Glasgow see never became an endowment for a royal bastard or the apanage of a noble house. But two great feudal families, the Stewarts of Darnley, whose chief was Earl of Lennox, and the Hamiltons, began to compete for mastery in the town.

The great cream-coloured fourteenth-century block of Crookston Castle, which was the Darnley Stewarts' chief home, now stands on its hill top between two new housing estates on the south-western outskirts of modern Glasgow. With its remaining square north-eastern tower, and its hall now laid open to the west wind, it is the most imposing of the medieval strongholds that the expanding city has absorbed. The Earl of Lennox, who was its lord in Archbishop Blacader's day, established himself as Provost of Glasgow and Bailie of the Regality—the manager of the Archbishop's lands and judge of his tenants. This earl led the men of Lennox and Glasgow to Flodden Field and died there beside his king. His descendants were apt to treat his Glasgow offices as hereditary: they were "servants of St. Mungo", but masterful servants. Between them, they and their Hamilton rivals carried Glasgow into the wars of the sixteenth century, the tragedy of Mary Stuart, and the crisis of the Reformation.

5 Crookston Castle, home of the Darnley Stewarts, Earls of Lennox

6 Provands Lordship, the oldest domestic building in central Glasgow (late fifteenth century)

7 The Cathedral and City from the Fir Park, now the Necropolis. T
The houses of the Drygate are in

8 The City from the South-
Both from engravings after John S.

"BEAUTIFULLEST LITTLE CIT

endinar Burn is on the left. Beyond the Cathedral is the Archbishop's Castle.
middle distance, with the College buildings behind them

wing the medieval Bridge
"*Theatrum Scotiae*", 1693

9, 10 Fifteenth-century interiors in what was once the manse of cathedral canons

PROVANDS LORDSHIP

CHAPTER THREE

Let Glasgow Flourish

1560 to 1690

FROM the hilltop which once was the Fir Park, opposite the cathedral, a colossal figure looks out over the church and the town. It is the figure of John Knox. It was set up in 1825, before the merchants of Glasgow decided to create around it a cemetery worthy of the city's wealth. The great reformer now stands above terraces of masonry, funerary temples, pagodas, rock tombs, aspiring angels—a vision from the City of Dreadful Night. To the men who made the Necropolis, it would have seemed fantastic that any other name than Knox's should open a chapter on the Reformation in Glasgow—the first great cataclysm in the city's history which shook the very roots of its existence by banishing saints from its worship and (for a while) bishops from its castle. In a sense our great-grandfathers were right. Though Knox's direct dealings with Glasgow were not very important it was he who set the mould for a good part of its future. Yet it is the figure of a lesser man which really stands at the beginning of the great change.

The Roman Church was already weakened in Scotland before the baby Mary Stuart became Queen of Scots. Its wealth had tempted kings and nobles to fill its high offices with their children. Its parish clergy were poor and unlearned. It set itself to fight the Lutheran doctrines from Germany: two Protestants, a Glasgow friar, Jerome Russell, and an Ayrshire youth of eighteen, John Kennedy, were condemned and burned beside Glasgow Cathedral in 1538. It had to fight England, too, for Henry VIII had pressed his nephew, James V, to follow him in breaking with the Pope. Now Henry hoped to get the little queen into his hands. The country was at a crisis when Matthew Stewart,

Earl of Lennox, the Archbishop's lay deputy in Glasgow, came home from France determined to be a very great man.

Lennox could not have been very great, for there was no greatness in him: even his name is scarcely remembered, though all subsequent kings of Scotland and Britain have been his descendants. He was a very important man, however, and the moment was one of those almost unnoticed ones in which history takes a decisive turn. He was second in succession to the throne. If his rival, the Earl of Arran, could be proved a bastard (as he claimed) he was the baby queen's heir. He was the spokesman of France and of Catholicism, captain of the French King's Guard, representative of a race of soldiers famous in Continental wars—Bernard Stewart, Duke of Terranuova, the Maréchal d'Aubigny. Though he had no loyalty to his faith or country he was capable of devoted attachment to a guiding woman. And he hoped to marry a very capable woman indeed, the Queen Mother, Mary of Lorraine.

If he had not been disappointed, the story of the Reformation in Scotland might have been radically changed—in Europe, too, perhaps, for Scotland was a decisive point in the struggle between Rome and the Reformers. He was a good soldier and might have given the two queens precisely the kind of support that they needed most. His success would surely have made Glasgow's history entirely different: the place would have remained either an archbishop's city or the capital of the wide Lennox lands. But the Roman Catholic leader, Cardinal David Beaton (nephew of one Glasgow archbishop and uncle of another), was, in this case, too clever for his own good. He thought that Lennox was safely on his side, whereas his Hamilton rival, Arran, half-Protestant and linked with England, must be bought over. So Lennox was encouraged and flattered but found himself deceived. Furiously, he turned to England. Henry VIII gave him his niece, Margaret Douglas, who ranked immediately after the Queen of Scots as the possible heiress of the English throne. Their son, Henry, Lord Darnley, was to be the ruin of Queen Mary, and, by merging the Lennox family in the royal one, was to end the possibility that Glasgow would become the apanage of a great feudal house.

For Glasgow, however, the more immediate result of Lennox's disappointment was a battle. It was called the Battle of the Butts because it was fought on the archery ground half a mile or so east of the Cross. The city was held for Lennox in 1544 when the Earl of Arran, now Governor of Scotland, attacked it. Lennox's force including Glasgow men under their provost, went out to fight and was defeated. The town was sacked: it was with difficulty that the enemy were persuaded not to burn it.

The Governor, who was made Duke of Chatelheurault in France, was now protector of the Archbishop, James Beaton, and his city. But the Reformation was gaining ground. The wavering Duke changed sides. In the last days of 1559, before a new settlement of religion had been formally established by a parliament of Reformers, the Archbishop rode out of Glasgow with an escort of French troops. Half a year later he carried the records and treasures of the diocese with him to France. He was to be the loyal ambassador of the Scottish sovereigns there for forty years, but his city was never to see him again. Suddenly, almost silently, medieval Glasgow had come to an end.

The cathedral choir was silent. The great church was stripped of images. The minor chapels of the city were deserted. The friaries were closed. But what is most striking in this revolution is the absence of violence. The "rascal multitude" which wrecked some other Scottish churches, the English raiders who destroyed many more, did not appear in Glasgow. Indeed, though there was a good deal of fighting and still more marching and counter-marching between the little armies of rival parties in Scotland during these years, persecutions and massacres of the kind seen in England, France, and Germany were strikingly few. Glasgow, we have seen, had two Protestant martyrs. It was to have one Roman Catholic one—the Jesuit John Ogilvie (beatified by his Church in our own day) who was burnt at the Cross in 1615, the only man to be publicly executed for that faith in Scotland.

No doubt many people on both sides suffered severely enough during the years of transition. But the priests and prelates of the old Church were still allowed (in theory, at least) to draw two-thirds of their old incomes as long as they lived: in Glasgow this must have meant that quite considerable revenues still flowed into the town, while a large part of the remaining Church funds were soon conveyed (again, perhaps, in theory rather than in practice, at first) to the University, the poor, and the Protestant ministers. The cathedral was saved from a threat of destruction by Glasgow folk themselves—by the embattled Trades, according to one story, by a very actively Protestant provost according to another.

One cannot avoid the impression that the old Church which had created Glasgow collapsed from its own weakness. There were very few Protestant preachers to take its place. For a while, the Superintendent of the West, John Willocks, carried on some of the archbishop's functions; and the city of Glasgow had a single Minister, David Wemyss. The University (what remained of it) was soon a strong focus of Protestantism. Yet in these years when the new Establishment seemed so weak, the religious life of Glasgow was transformed. A handful of Roman Catholics remained in John Ogilvie's day, but Glasgow was as effectively Protestant then as it has been since.

By the end of the sixteenth century, too, the city was evidently growing fast: it had, perhaps, 4,500 people in 1560, and 7,600 in 1610. Its trade had, in fact, been swelling when the great change came. Its market, wrote the Catholic Bishop Lesley, "sends to the East country very fat cattle, herring and salmon, ox-hides, wool and skins, the best of butter and cheese", with "all kinds of corn" to the western lowlands, and to Argyll and the Isles, wine, ale, aqua-vitae, and other drinks. The city, he wrote, is "beautifully placed and pleasant, abounding with garden stuff, apple trees and orchards".

For a while the upper parts of the town, where the clergy had lived, was threatened with decay, but even this sort of depression seems to have passed by 1596, for, when it was suggested, during a political crisis, that the supreme courts should be transferred from Edinburgh the Town Council appears to have shown very little interest in the idea: Glasgow seems, in fact, to have thrown away its one chance of becoming the capital of Scotland.

History had confirmed its position as the capital of the West, however. When Mary Queen of Scots came home, a girlish widow, to rule her own country in 1562, the Earl of Lennox soon followed her. His powers in Glasgow were restored to him, but his chief object was to marry her to his son—now, by one of the odd changes of the time, the chief hope of the English Catholics. The boy, Darnley, was no more than a handsome lout, but he was soon King consort of Scotland and Glasgow was the centre of what power he and his family had in the country. Legend says that the Queen was with him at Crookston: there was an ancient yew-tree there, under which they were believed to have talked together. The city itself saw Mary at more than one of the crises of her story. She was there, happy and glorious, with her newly married husband beside her when Glasgow was the rendezvous of the troops with which she scattered her enemies during the Chaseabout Raid. When Darnley's faithlessness had broken his marriage and lost him all his supporters, the Queen came to visit him as he lay sick in the Lennox town house opposite the cathedral. Mary's accusers insisted that the letter—almost certainly faked—in which she seems to prepare for his murder, was written on a day of this Glasgow January of 1567.

Less than a year and a half later, her bastard brother, the Earl of Moray, now Regent for her baby son, was holding court in Glasgow when he learned that the Queen had escaped from her imprisonment in Lochleven. He summoned his forces there while her supporters were gathering at Hamilton, ten miles away. Moray imagined that the Queen's army of 6,000 men would try to force its way along the north bank of the Clyde to the fortress of Dumbarton, from which she could have had a link by sea with France or Spain. Instead they moved south of the river. Mounting a foot soldier behind each of his horsemen, Moray sent his troops across the famous eight-arched bridge (the pride of Glasgow for centuries, but so narrow that two could scarcely ride abreast) to occupy Camphill, with its medieval earthwork, two miles to the south.

The decisive battle of the Reformation wars was fought over what are now the streets and gardens of the Victorian suburb of Langside. The Queen's men tried to force their way to the hill top where the battle monument now stands. But Moray's general,

49

Kirkcaldy of Grange, lined the hedges about the road there with hagbutters, the musketeers of the time. The Queen's men broke under the fire. They were pursued and scattered on the lower ground that is now called Battlefield. Mary, who had been watching the fight, probably from the Court Knowe of Cathcart, beside the modern Lynn Park a mile or so away, rode south towards the Solway. On 14th May, 1568, she took refuge in England. Twenty years of imprisonment and her execution at Fotheringay lay before her.

Glasgow was on the winning side in this battle. Since the little King, James VI, was a grandson of Lennox, the local chieftain, the burgesses seem to have favoured the Regent. Six hundred Glasgow men fought for him. And the town did not suffer when, after Moray's murder, Lennox himself became Regent, though he began a process which in the end was to make it impossible for Glasgow to develop into a Protestant York.

This was the appointment of "tulchan"* bishops, whose chief function was to convey revenues and lands to their patrons, as a stuffed calf-skin (tulchan) would induce a cow to yield to the milk-maid. Such men had no real place in the Church, but since their titles gave them seats in the Estates (the Scots Parliament) they could be useful politically. A series of phantom archbishops now flits across the Glasgow scene, providing their patrons with some benefit from the revenues or lands of the see, placing suitable nominees in local offices, struggling with the Presbyterian courts of the Church, whose position grew stronger as the tulchans showed their inadequacy, and sometimes disappearing tactfully when the great men behind them fell from power.

In the later years before he became King of England, and still more forcibly after he found himself Supreme Head of an episcopal Church beyond the Border, James VI made a real effort to convert these shadow-bishops into genuine rulers of their dioceses on the English pattern. The last but one of his archbishops of Glasgow, John Spottiswoode, was an ecclesiastical

---

* This nickname, which comes to us from James Melville's *Diary*, is now out of fashion with historians, but so far as the See of Glasgow is concerned its appropriateness can scarcely be questioned.

civil servant of real character, ability, and learning. He is unlucky enough to be remembered for his share (a predominant one) in the prosecution of the Roman Catholic martyr, the Blessed John Ogilvie, but he was not a violent man, though he was an authoritative one, and he did what he could to build up both his see and his city. If Scotland had known Protestant bishops of his kind in the early years of the Reformation it is possible that the Presbyterian structure of her national Church might never have become firmly rooted. But by his time bishops, in the eyes of most Scotsmen, were rather ludicrous figures who ceased to be contemptible only when they became dangerous as agents for a King who was attempting to anglicise what had become the national Kirk—and, incidentally, to recover Church lands and revenues from powerful laymen. When Archbishop Spottiswoode left Glasgow for St. Andrews the first ripples of a new religious struggle which would fill the century were breaking on the Scottish scene. His own appointment as Chancellor of Scotland was later to alarm and shock the great nobles, who thought that the Reformation had freed them from the competition of episcopal statesmen.

About this time the city began to find a motto for itself, which was also an invocation—"Lord, let Glasgow flourish by the preaching of the Word and praising Thy Name". There was preaching now from four or five pulpits perhaps four times a week, and prayer in almost every household. Materially, Glasgow was flourishing. It had equipped itself with a new constitution. Its merchants were grouped under an elected magistrate, the Dean of Guild, and his court "according to the lovable form of jugement usit in all the guid tounis of France and Flanderis". The craftsmen were organised in Incorporations, federated under a Deacon Convener, and the privileges of their Trades House and the Merchants House carefully regulated by a charter from the Town Council, the Letter of Guildry of 1605, which still governs these bodies, now transformed into respected middle-class friendly societies. The Town Council itself had probably ceased to be elected by the assembly of burgesses some time in the fifteenth century. It would now consist of merchants and craftsmen nominated by a sort of electoral college of magistrates and ex-magistrates (the provost and bailies of three successive years) who had themselves been confirmed in office by the archbishop— or whoever held the archbishop's powers during years of confusion.

As the population grew, stone "lands" or tenements began to appear along the chief streets round the Cross, which were wide enough to be used as market-places. And the little city sprouted towers and spires. Three of these still give a character to the older streets, otherwise almost completely transformed in the last century and a half.

At the Cross itself is the Tolbooth Steeple, now a square, isolated tower, unnaturally slim since the handsome seventeenth-century Town House to which it belonged has disappeared. Its heavy Gothic crown, on a model once greatly favoured in Scotland, holds the "music bells", too seldom heard now, that played out over Glasgow for three centuries.

On the other side of the open space, now broken by Sir John Burnet's surprisingly apt little railway station, the Tron spire, also seventeenth-century Gothic, spans the pavement. It belonged to a sixteenth-century church—before the Reformation, the College of St. Mary and St. Ann, and later the first Reformed Kirk of the lower town. The plain, square, but charmingly proportioned Adam building which replaced the first church after a fire is now a municipal workshop.

The third, and perhaps the most attractive, of these towers is still an unmistakable feature of the Glasgow skyline as seen from the bridges, with its Dutch-looking details and the ship weather-vane, emblem of the Merchants, that completes it. It was, in fact, the steeple of the handsome baroque Merchants' Hall in the Briggate, though it now presides over the not unsympathetic façade of the Victorian fish-market. Hall and steeple were probably designed by Sir William Bruce.

A fourth steeple, at least equally handsome, was destroyed when the University abandoned its fine old home in the High Street to a railway company. This, too, belonged to the mid-seventeenth century, as did a fifth, now lost, the steeple of Hutcheson's Hospital.

All these were built when the "preaching of the word" pre-occupied Glasgow men quite as seriously as their interest in material wealth, which was serious enough. George Hutcheson was as typical a figure of the years between the Reformation troubles and the wars of the Covenant as one can find. He belonged to a class that supplied the city with many of its merchants, lawyers and provost for generations after his day. They were descendants of the "rentallers", who worked the bishop's lands. Most of these families had held their farms for centuries. Because they were so close to the city markets, they were apt to be prosperous farmers. Under the tulchan arch-bishops or the lay lords who sometimes supplanted them, many of the rentallers bought their lands and emerged as small lairds.

One remaining house on the eastern fringe of modern Glasgow gives us an idea of what their homes may have been like. To be sure, Provan Hall* was more than a rentaller's house. It was, the country seat of the prebendaries of Barlanark, the centre of their lands of Provan. The fifteenth- or sixteenth-century block which survives, with its heavily vaulted ground floor and its "pepper-box" stair tower, pierced for defence, must have been built about the same time as Provand's Lordship. It may even have sheltered the royal canon, James IV. Joined to a second block by a massive curtain wall, it was, in the seventeenth century, the house of a knightly family. But in its modest strength, its solid Scotsness, under its grove of beeches, the older part of Provan Hall is probably very much the sort of place that the more prosperous of the little Glasgow lairds would have chosen for themselves.

The Hutcheson family was already prospering before George, the eldest son, could call himself laird of Lambhill, now a northern suburb. Before he died, he owned half a dozen other small estates or farms in or about modern Glasgow. He was certainly not a saint, being a little given to violence and un-expected fatherhood, but he was a man with a conscience as well as a native capacity for gathering wealth.

Born just before the Reformation was established, he became

* Now under the care of the National Trust for Scotland.

a lawyer (procurator and notary public) in the city, helping to dispose of the archbishops' lands, acting for the Town Council and the University, buying himself the (apparently) lucrative office of judge-depute in the Commissary Courts of Glasgow and Hamilton—the old ecclesiastical courts which, in Glasgow at least, also dealt with most civil cases. And he was what would now be called a private banker, perhaps the first in the city. He lent money to half the lairds and nobles of the west and even to the city itself—the impressive spring-locked chest in which he kept his charters, bonds and cash is in the Procurators' library.

When he died in 1639 most of his riches went to his much younger brother, Thomas, and with them the duty to establish a hospital, near his house in the Trongate, for eleven aged men. Thomas added enough money and property to lodge and educate ten boys, orphans of burgesses, as well. From this has grown the Hutcheson Trust, which supports two famous grammar schools, one for boys and one for girls, besides administering other charities. Hutcheson Street marks the site of the original hospital. At the head of it a neat, spired building by David Hamilton, faintly reminiscent of the seventeenth century in spite of its classicism, houses the Trust's offices and displays contemporary figures of the two pious brothers on its façade.

Pious they were. The end of this success story shows Thomas Hutcheson at the head of those who helped to finance Glasgow's contribution to the first of the Covenanting armies. The peace in which Glasgow had flourished so equably was breaking when his brother George died.

James VI and I had set up bishops who, according to his plans, were to be taken seriously. He had silenced the Presbyterian leaders who told him that he was "God's sillie vassel", in Christ's kingdom "nocht a king, nor a lord, nor a heid, but a member",★ and had insisted on his own supremacy over the Scottish Church as well as over the English one. His son, Charles I, went further. He reclaimed Church lands from their lay holders and tried to impose the Anglican service and Anglican usages on Scotland. The result was the explosion of the National Covenant.

★ The words are Andrew Melville's. See Chapter VIII.

The country was prepared for resistance. In Glasgow the Town Council bought arms and drilled volunteers. Embarrassed in his dealings with his English Parliament and unable to suppress the movement by force, Charles agreed to allow a free General Assembly of the Kirk—one not dominated by the bishops and the king's Commissioner as recent assemblies had been. It was to meet in Glasgow and a free Parliament was to be held in Edinburgh.

It may have been thought that in Glasgow, the city of the King's Lennox ancestors and close to the estates of his Commissioner, the Marquis of Hamilton, the atmosphere would be friendly to his claims. But Glasgow was, very definitely, for the Covenant. The Assembly of 1638 met in the cathedral, where the triphorium passages and wooden galleries specially built for this occasion were packed with spectators. The members, ministers and lay elders proceeded to condemn the bishops. Hamilton declared it dissolved, but it sat on. The whole ecclesiastical system set up by the King and his father was voted down. A revolution had begun, and the long civil wars.

In a sense, the town was still extraordinarily lucky during thirteen years of violence and fifty of political trouble. The provost who had been captain of Glasgow's troops at the beginning of the wars and hoped to blow up the victorious Oliver Cromwell at the end of them turned out to be a skilful, daring (and honest) investor, who acquired for it, and Hutcheson's Hospital, the valuable (if now too famous) lands of Gorbals, just south of the river. Victorious enemies treated Glasgow with surprising gentleness—Montrose, after his last success at Kilsyth, twelve miles away, drawing tears of gratitude from magistrates who had expected a sack of the city, and withdrawing his Irish and Highlanders when they showed a tendency to plunder; Cromwell himself listening peaceably to a denunciation from the pulpit of the Barony Kirk (the lower church of the cathedral) and then holding the preacher, Zachary Boyd,* in prayer for

---

* Boyd left most of his fortune to the university of which he had been Rector and Vice-Chancellor, on condition that it should publish his works, including quantities of scriptural verse. The money was taken, but the books have not appeared.

three hours. As one crisis followed another, there was a whole series of minor revolutions among the magistrates, but never any horrifying act of vengeance. Accidents of fire apart, Glasgow suffered no real destruction.

Yet the high moments of history touched it, and the sort of drama and disappointment that must have wrung the hearts of thousands of its people. For twelve years the streets rang with the march of drilling men, of Scots troops on their way to the English wars, of citizens going out to dig a great defensive ditch round the town, of Montrose's Royalists, Baillie's Covenanters, Hamilton's Engagers, the Cromwellian army of occupation. For three years, plague raged in the city. Financially it was almost ruined when the fighting ended.

To Scots Presbyterians, to Glasgow merchants and men like the Hutchesons, who, no doubt, believed that a country in which the Word was preached would flourish in the ways most obvious to themselves, these years brought an appalling disappointment. Scotland had fought not merely for the right to worship in the way most of its people thought right, but to save the King himself from error and to establish true religion in England and Ireland. It had been a colossal and exhausting effort, and through most of the years of crisis it had seemed to be successful. Scots armies had seldom been defeated except by Scotsmen themselves.

Yet, in the end, after Cromwell's last victories, Scotland was more completely at the mercy of the English than she had been for more than three centuries. Her Church was powerless, King Charles (a Scotsman) was dead and his son in exile. Glasgow men did not lose their determination that the city must flourish: the national spirit did not die, but it began to change. The religious struggle was to revive in the west, though it was a wilder, more sectional thing, no longer the effort of an organised nation. But another and now quite separate effort was gathering too—a determined struggle for wealth. Even during the Cromwellian occupation and in the depressing years of the Restoration that followed—when, for the first time, Glasgow's population actually fell—one can see the beginning of an unrelenting campaign to make the city flourish, not as the ecclesiastical centre of the west,

11   Glasgow Cross in 1820. The Tolbooth steeple and Tontine Hotel
on the right. The Tron Steeple on the left
From the painting by John Knox in the Old Glasgow Museum

12   The Archbishops' Castle and Glasgow Cathedral. The Cathedral's
Western Tower and Consistory House were destroyed 1846–48
*Engraved by Joseph Swan (in ''Select Views of Glasgow'', 1828) from
a drawing of 1790*

13 Provan Hall: a late medieval country house with seventeenth- and
eighteenth-century additions

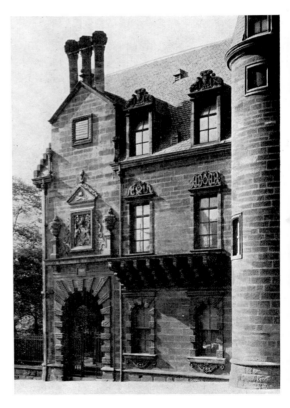

14 Old Merchants
House Steeple, Bridge-
gate (*Sir William Bruce,*
architect)

15 Pearce Lodge, Glasgow University: the
reconstructed façade of the Old College

but as a great place of trade—to overcome the natural disadvantages of its situation, to open the door to a wider world.

Irvine harbour, the Hull of the little Scottish York, was
silting up. Other long-established towns—Ayr and Dumbarton,
particularly—could have taken its place as the chief sea-port of
the Clyde. But it was Glasgow which set itself, against all
difficulties, to dominate the sea routes to the west. Before the
wars, the Town Council had already tried to deepen the Clyde
at the shallows of Dumbuck, and so open a sea-going passage.
When this failed, it prepared to create an entirely new port for
itself at Fairlie, in North Ayrshire.

Almost as soon as the fighting was over, foreign trade began to
develop. A Cromwellian official, Thomas Tucker, who was sent
to Scotland in 1655 to help to make arrangements for customs
and excise, was impressed by Glasgow. "This towne", he wrote,
"seated in a pleasant and fruitfull soyle, and consisting of foure
streets, handsomely built in forme of a crosse, is one of the most
considerablest burghs of Scotland, as well for the structure as
trade of it. The inhabitants (all but the students of the colledge
which is here) are traders and dealers: some for Ireland with small
smiddy coales, in open boates, from foure to ten tonnes, from
whence they bring hoopes, ronges, barrell staves, meale, oates
and butter; some from France with pladding, coales, and herring,
(of which there is a greate fishing yearly in the Westerne Sea)
for which they return salt, paper, rosin, and prunes; some to
Norway for timber; and every one with theyr neighbours the
Highlanders, who come hither from the isles and westerne parts;
in summer by the Mul of Cantyre, and in winter by the Torban
[Tarbert] to the head of the Loquh Fyn (which is a small neck of
sandy land, over which they usually draw theyr small boates into
the Firth of Dunbarton) and soe passe up in the Cluyde with
pladding, dry hides, goate, kid, and deere skyns, which they sell,
and purchase with theyr price such commodities and provisions
as they stand in neede of, from time to time.

"Here hath likewise beene some who have adventured as farre
as the Barbadoes; but the losse they have sustayned by reason of
theyr goeing out and comeing home late every yeare, have made

them discontinue goeing thither any more. The scituation of this towne in a plentifull land, and the mercantile genius of the people, are strong signes of her increase and groweth, were she not checqued and kept under by the shallownesse of her river, every day more and more increasing and filling up, soe that noe vessells of any burden can come neerer up then within fourteene miles, where they must unlade, and send up theyr timber, and Norway trade in rafts on floats, and all other comodotyes, by three or foure tonnes of goods at a time, in small cobbles or boates of three, foure, five, and none of above six tonnes, a boate.''

A former soldier of Cromwell, Richard Franck, was even more enthusiastic—''What to think, or what to say of this eminent Glasgow, I know not, except to fancy a smell of my native country. The very prospect of this flourishing city reminds me of the beautiful fabricks and the florid fields in England. . . . How many such cities shall we meet with in our travels, where the streets and the channels are so cleanly swept, and the meat in every house so artificially drest? The linen, I also observed, was very neatly lap'd up, and, to their praise be it spoke, was lavender proof; besides, the people were decently drest, and such an exact decorum in every society, represents it, to my apprehension, an emblem of England, though, in some measure, under a deeper die. However, I'le superscribe it to the nonsuch of Scotland, where an English florist may pick up a posie; so that should the residue of their cities, in our northern progress, seem as barren as uncultivated fields, and every field so replenished with thistles that a flower could scarcely flourish amongst them, yet would I celebrate thy praise, O, Glasgow! because of those pleasant and fragrant flowers that so sweetly refresh'd me, and, to admiration, sweetned our present enterments.''★

When Charles II was welcomed home, the search for an effective harbour continued. The first plan had not proved workable, but in 1668, Glasgow finally began to build one for itself at Newark, where the Firth of Clyde opened, 20 miles

★ Both these impressions of Glasgow are found in *Early Travellers in Scotland* edited by P. Hume Brown.

away. The new Port Glasgow was to be the centre of its sea-going trade for the best part of two centuries.

There was a whole series of lesser experiments in trade, industry and social comfort, most of them backed by the Town Council, or even the Privy Council—for Charles II's Scottish Governments were almost as keenly interested in such things as the Glasgow burgesses themselves. Cloth factories, a soapworks, a sugar refinery, a candle industry were set up—the latter is commemorated in a street name, Candleriggs. The first coffee-house was established (with a monopoly) and the Town Council even supported a sort of municipal restaurant. It also subsidised a weekly coach service to Edinburgh and cabs (hackney coaches) in the city itself. Some of these efforts collapsed fairly quickly, but they forecast the shape of the next century.

There was a very much darker side to these years, however. The Restoration brought the archbishops back. In a sense they were more powerful than any of their predecessors since the Reformation: some of them were certainly more assertive. One, Robert Leighton, was as near to being a saint as any successor of St. Mungo's. But in the eyes of the people they were now the privileged leaders of an ecclesiastical party, and one not much respected in the west of Scotland.

The hearts of most the pious were still with the Covenants, which Charles II had once accepted but now abhorred. In these documents, Scotland had made a sort of treaty with God which, Presbyterian enthusiasts believed, must never be denied.

Charles's rule began in Glasgow with a University revolution and the meeting in the College Forehall of the "Drunken Parliament", a committee of Privy Councillors which decided to drive Covenanting ministers from their churches. Outlawed conventicles heard the preaching of the Word on neighbouring moors and hillsides, and even (often enough) in the heart of the city itself. A Highland Host of clansmen passed south to repress the western Whigs—the Covenanters of the neighbouring shires —and, on its return, is said to have had to surrender some of its spoils to a mob of red-gowned students who waited for it at Glasgow Bridge. Through a June day of 1679, royal troops lay behind barricades in the High Street and the Gallowgate expecting the attack of the rebel hill-men after their victory at Drumclog. The Covenanters withdrew. Their rebellion was easily broken. But Glasgow and the West Country still seethed with frustrated enthusiasm.

"Glasgow", says the Rev. Thomas Morer, an Englishman who visited it in its last episcopal days, "is a place of great extent and good situation; and has the reputation of the finest town in Scotland, not excepting Edinburgh, tho' the royal city. This cathedral, with one large church more in the heart of the city where the magistrates attend, are all the places of publick worship in Glasgow, the nest of fanaticism, and the most factious town in all that kingdom. . . . Here are several hospitals, or houses of charity, and many spires more for ornament than use: And a tolbooth or common-hall very magnificent (as most of 'em are in the towns of Scotland) for publick entertainments, or city business.

"Glasgow is as factious as it is rich. Yet the most considerable persons for quality, are well disposed to the church. But the disaffected make up that defect with number, and sometimes call the hill men or field conventiclers to assist 'em."

In 1684, the city itself saw its martyrs—five of them died at the Cross "in much comfort, peace and the utmost cheerfulness" and three more at the Howgate Head, just north of the archbishop's castle—a stone in Castle Street marks their burial place. Another inscription, preserved in the cathedral, has its comment on the pursuers and executioners:

> They'll find at Resurrection Day
> To murder saints was no sweet play.

From the point of view of the King and his Government, the "saints" were certainly rebels or sympathisers with rebellion. But the popular point of view of Glasgow is faithfully echoed in the tombstone's grim doggerel.

The Town Council of those years was dominated by the Crown or successive Archbishops who, as their influence weakened, interfered in municipal affairs more recklessly than any of their predecessors. When the last Stuart King, James VII and II, was threatened by the Whig revolutionaries, the Glasgow magistrates raised 1,200 men to support him. But the recruits refused to leave the city. On the other hand, 500 could be found in one day to support the new Government of William of Orange and form the nucleus of the famous Cameronian Regiment. The last of the phantom archbishops★ was blown away with the last king of the old race. Glasgow was already the second city of Scotland, a town without a lord, seeking its own destiny. A little later, the century-old motto, suitably shortened, was formally attached to the municipal coat of arms. It now read simply "Let Glasgow Flourish".

★ The bishopric of Glasgow and Galloway of the Episcopal Church in Scotland was permanently re-established in 1837, the Roman Catholic archbishopric in 1878.

CHAPTER FOUR

The Merchant Town

1690 to 1780

"THESE limes," said Sir Walter Scott's Bailie Nicol Jarvie, when he sat down to make a bowl of punch in his Glasgow flat, "these limes are from my own little farm yonder-awa." The farm was a plantation in the West Indies. The bailie was a well-doing, Sabbath-keeping magistrate and business man, a conscious model of common sense and respectability. He was also (presumably) a slave owner. And he was the cousin of a Highland chieftain, deep in the intrigue and violence of the Jacobite half-world. Perhaps no figure in Glasgow's history was exactly like Scott's bailie, yet the spirit of Glasgow just a little more than two centuries ago is wonderfully caught in the chapters of *Rob Roy* which describe him. It is the spirit of an outpost where two (or three) worlds meet.

Through most of its past Glasgow has been at the edge of a world. It was the farthest city of the feudal Franco-British world which stretched west from the Alps. From its very streets, even in the early eighteenth century, its burgesses could see hills that lay beyond that world—where a strange language, Gaelic, was spoken and the ancient life of the clans still existed. It was also (as it still is) the last great gateway of civic Europe towards the New World beyond the ocean. By the middle of the eighteenth century, when transatlantic trade was flourishing triumphantly, America seemed as close and familiar, in the consciousness of Glasgow citizens, as London was; and they were a great deal more conscious of London than they had been in the archbishops' days. Glasgow still has a suburb, Mount Vernon, which got its name from the home not of President Washington, the father of the American Republic, but of his elder brother, Laurence

Washington, who was a friend and neighbour in Virginia of the Glasgow Mount Vernon's first proprietor at a time when Major George Washington was simply a distinguished colonial soldier.

There is a wide gap, one would say, between this state of things and the Glasgow life of the seventeenth century, though it is a gap of only sixty years or so. Certainly decisive things had happened in that lifetime. The most decisive was the union of the Scots and English Parliaments in which the ancient Scottish State disappeared.

That had followed the failure of a supreme effort to find an independent place for Scotland in the new system of transatlantic trade and colonial empires. The Scots, who were desperately short of wealth—of actual coined money—at the end of nearly a century of war and several years of famine, had put almost everything they had into national Company Trading to Africa and the Indies, which attempted to seize and hold a place at one of the great cross-roads of the world, the Isthmus of Darien, where the Panama Canal runs now. Glasgow men subscribed £56,000 sterling to the Company. That was probably more money than its 12,000 citizens could actually have laid hands on. When mis-management and English and Spanish opposition wrecked the plan and a handful of surviving colonists staggered back to the Clyde Scotland was, in fact, practically bankrupt.

For Scotsmen, the great promise of the plan of Union with England was that it would offset this colossal disappointment by opening up trade with the English colonies. Yet the plan was intensely unpopular, even in Glasgow where hopes of trans-atlantic trade had been growing for half a century.

"Up and be valiant for the city of our God", cried a preacher in the Tron Kirk. The town rose. The Articles of Union were burnt at the Cross. The Provost fled to Edinburgh. The Tolbooth was seized. An armed party from Glasgow marched east, expect-ing to find a national force which was said to be massing for the defence of the Kirk and Scottish parliamentary independence. But this army did not gather. Early in December, 1706, the Glasgow riots subsided. On 16th January, 1707, the Scots Parliament finally passed the Act of Union.

It is sometimes suggested that Glasgow's trade began to flourish noticeably almost at once. But this does not seem to have been so. The merchants certainly tried to take advantage of their new opportunities. But this competition was very badly received in England. When Glasgow showed signs of capturing a share in the American tobacco trade, the English importing interests, putting strong pressure on the Government, made feverish and, at first, not unsuccessful efforts to check this advance. The Scots linen trade, which was the country's chief export industry, was also heavily attacked.

Glasgow's discontent finally blew up in 1725, when a new tax on ale was imposed. Before the Union, Scots burghs could seldom complain that their commissioners in the Estates had failed to represent them properly, for these M.P.s were delegates of the town councils who chose, paid and controlled them. In the British House of Commons, however, Glasgow shared one representative with Dumbarton, Rutherglen and Renfrew. Duncan Campbell of Shawfield, a prosperous and powerful merchant, was believed to have acted against his constituents' interests and wishes not only over the Malt Tax but also in connection with the tobacco trade. A mob gathered to demonstrate against the tax. Campbell's fine new house in the Trongate, "the Shawfield Mansion", was sacked. Troops fired on the people at the Cross and nine were killed. An enraged Government threw the provost and magistrates into jail—there is no doubt that some of them at least had a good deal of sympathy with the rioters. In the end, two of the mob leaders were banished and the fortunate Mr. Campbell received the enormous sum of £8,680 as compensation at the expense of the town. With this he bought the islands of Islay and Jura, which his clan had acquired after more than a century of Machiavellian diplomacy and war.

However, the truly flourishing and peaceful Glasgow of Bailie Nicol Jarvie was now about to be born. In the eyes of travellers, it was already a remarkably pleasant place.

"The beautifullest little city I have seen in Britain", wrote Daniel Defoe.* "It stands deliciously on the banks of the river

* In *A Journey Through Scotland*, 1723

Clyde. . . . The four principal streets", he added later, "are the fairest for breadth and the finest built that I have ever seen in one city together. The houses are all of stone, and generally uniform in height as well as in front. The lower storeys for the most part stand on vast Doric columns with arches which open into the shops, adding to the strength as well as the beauty of the building."

These arcades, known as *piazzas* in Scotland, were in fact confined to the streets about the Cross, which was now entirely surrounded by tall stone tenements or "lands". They made a strong impression on all visitors. Their effect must have been a little like what one still sees in the Rue de Rivoli, though the buildings above them were less regular. At the Cross, a treasured statue of William of Orange, the gift of the first Scots nabob, a governor of Madras, boldly bestrode a spirited steed. You will find it now in Cathedral Square, tactfully screened by trees from demonstrators who used to make it a rallying point on the Twelfth of July.

Beyond the piazzas and the stone lands, however, there were older, wooden-fronted houses in the High Street and Saltmarket, and in the upper town the medieval manses still looked out on their gardens. The whole place must have had a rather collegiate air, for Hutcheson's Hospital and the Merchants' House repeated, in a small way, the pattern of the University. In 1736, McUre, the first historian of Glasgow, was to write of "the pleasant and odoriferous smell" of flowers and fruit, which filled "the open and large streets".

Other smells, to be sure, must have been present there too, from time to time, for, in spite of repeated orders of the Town Council, burgesses still left their dung and refuse to accumulate under the open sky till it could be carted away for manure. On the whole, however, Glasgow was an orderly place, and not over-crowded. It was not till later in the century that many open spaces began to be filled up with more closely set buildings, or that the whipping round the town of minor criminals convicted by the bailies became a public show on almost every market day.

"I have not heard either of a house or a head broken, of a

pocket picked or any other flagrant crime since I came here'',
wrote the great philosopher of ''common sense'', Thomas Reid,
in 1764. ''I have not heard any swearing in the streets, nor seen
a man drunk (excepting *inter nos*, one professor).'' This was more
than half a century after the severe and simple days when a
dancing teacher was allowed by the Town Council to establish
himself only on condition that he behaved soberly, and allowed
''noe promiscuous dancing of young men and women together,
but that each sex shall be taught by themselves, and that one sex
shall be dismissed and out of his home before the other enters
therein''. Glasgow remained, on the whole, frugal and well-
behaved, but wealth was giving it a more liberal way of life,
though Thomas Reid could complain that the ''common people'',
however law-abiding, were ''Boeotian in their understandings,
fanatical in their religion and churlish in their dress and manners.
The clergy'', he added, ''encourage this fanaticism too much,
and find it the only way to popularity.''★

The simple life of the town's leaders is described by Alexander
Carlyle, who, full of the sophistication or Edinburgh, calls it coarse
and vulgar—''The principal merchants, fatigued with the morn-
ings business, took an early dinner with their families at home,
and then resorted to the coffeehouse or tavern to read the newspapers, which they generally did in companies of four or five in
separate rooms, over a bottle of claret or a bowl of punch. But
they never staid supper, but always went home by nine o'clock,
without company or further amusement. At last an arch fellow
from Dublin, a Mr. Cockaine, came to be master of the chief
coffeehouse, who seduced them gradually to stay supper by
placing a few nice cold things at first on the table, as relishers to
the wine, till he gradually led them on to bespeak fine hot suppers,
and to remain till midnight.

''There was an order of women at that time in Glasgow, who,
being either young widows not wealthy, or young women un-
provided for, were set up in small grocery-shops in various parts
of the town, and generally were protected and countenanced by
some creditable merchant. In their back shops much time and

★ Letter to Dr. David Skene, 18th July, 1765.

money were consumed; for it being customary then to drink drams and white wine in the forenoon, the tipplers resorted much to these shops, where there were bedrooms; and the patron, with his friends, frequently passed the evening there also, as taverns were not frequented by persons who affected characters of strict decency."*

What made the Glasgow of Bailie Nicol Jarvie was the sudden growth of trade. Even before the Union, its merchants had managed, one way or another, to import sugar and tobacco across the Atlantic. The great gift that the new link with England brought them—once the opposition of Bristol and other towns had been broken—was a share in what was practically a world monopoly. Direct dealings between the future United States and the continent of Europe was forbidden. And the American colonies were the world's chief source of tobacco. A firm hold on this traffic was bound to give Glasgow an unfailing business not only with the new world but with European ports as well. Helped a little by wars which interfered with the shipping of the southern ports, the Clyde merchants drew in more and more of the tobacco trade till their share in it was the largest in the world.

Sugar, too, flowed in from the West Indies. Two Scots officers in the island of St. Kitts, Colonel William MacDowall and Major James Milliken, married the heiresses of great plantations there and brought their brides and their wealth back to Scotland. In 1727 MacDowall bought the Shawfield Mansion, still the one great new house in the city, and he and his friend established a flourishing sugar business.

This was, perhaps, the first flush of transatlantic riches to make a decisive impact on Glasgow life. And not on Glasgow only. The ships that brought home sugar and tobacco must take out goods to pay for them. New factories began to appear around the city itself—for leather, soap, glass, nails. And throughout Scotland linen-making was being revived and improved. The British Government was at last persuaded to use some otherwise unexpended Scots funds for this purpose. Clyde ships could now

* *Autobiography,* Chapter III.

take all the linen that was fit for sale to market in the colonies. Coarse Scottish cloth made shirts for slaves, and the finer linens woven near Glasgow itself for their masters. A reviving, stimulating stream of money gushed into the country.

Money, actual coin, had been desperately needed. Scotland was not, by nature, a particularly poor country. Except in rare years when the crops failed, its people had usually been adequately fed and clothed. But the long wars before the Union and the drain of taxation to the south after it had left it painfully short of the means of buying and selling. The first banks succeeded partly because their notes filled this gap. But in 1728, a future Provost of Glasgow, Andrew Cochrane, was able to embarrass the Bank of Scotland very severely by demanding £900 in hard cash. Edinburgh was, and remained, the main financial centre, though after 1750 Glasgow had banks of its own, with Andrew Cochrane himself as the chief partner in one of them. It was through Glasgow, however, that the new wealth came which transformed not only the towns of Scotland but its fields in the years of agricultural improvement.

And in Glasgow, this was the first great age not only of money-making but of thought about business—of the formation of ideas which were to guide the city's leaders long after the tobacco trade itself had died away. The voice of this thought was Adam Smith, who was Professor of Moral Philosophy in the University from 1752 to 1764. His book *The Wealth of Nations* is perhaps the most decisive, the most deeply influential piece of writing ever to come out of Scotland. In a sense it is the greatest Glasgow book. Though very little of it may have been written in Glasgow, many of its theories surely grew there.

In spite, perhaps because, of their lack of money, many educated and politically minded Scots had shown an intense interest in economic affairs since the days of the Covenant Wars. About the beginning of the eighteenth century the Keyneses of England and France, the men who worked out new plans for expanding credit and trade and sought to apply them, were both Scots, William Paterson and John Law. In Glasgow, a tradition of economic theorising in the University's philosophy classes established itself while the councillors and merchants were struggling to open their river and push their trade. Adam Smith was the heir to these things. It was at Glasgow that he saw the actual working of an adventurous and expanding economy. It was there, too, that he heard the problems of trade discussed, first as a student under Francis Hutcheson, a philosophic Whig (or Radical) whose teaching had the deepest possible influence on the minds of Scots intellectuals, and then as a friend of Andrew Cochrane. He was a member of Cochrane's club, in which leading merchants met weekly to "inquire into the principles of trade".

Eighteenth-century Glasgow was a city of such clubs—not societies with buildings of their own, but gatherings for discussion and conviviality. Smith belonged to at least two others where professors might meet the most intelligent leaders of the town.

In these gatherings, Glasgow had something a little like the famous Lunar Society where the great men of Birmingham met to re-cast the world a generation later. Perhaps city and university have never owed so much to one another as they did in the middle of the eighteenth century. Because many of the merchants and magistrates had passed through the College, discussion between them and the extraordinarily talented group of professors who had gathered there was easy. The views of Adam Smith, which were to influence traders and governments for generations, were familiar in Glasgow while the rest of the world was just beginning to learn about them. Long after Smith had left them, Glasgow business men could feel that they knew the way through the new age of manufacturing industry and world commerce while others were feeling, rather blindly, for the right path. Perhaps the time has been when Glasgow found itself rather too thoroughly steeped in Smithian doctrine for its own material good, but that was long after the life of the eighteenth century had faded from men's minds.

A few years before Adam Smith came back to teach in the High Street, Glasgow had had a visitation which, to those who had known it and looked back on it, must have had an almost spectral quality. The booming, growing commercial city had seen the past in its own streets. The Jacobite adventure of the Forty-five might, indeed, have changed the course of history if it had been pushed to the end as boldly as its leader planned, but though Prince Charlie's march through Scotland, his victories and his final defeat, created many fears and problems for Presbyterian Glasgow, they scarcely affected the city's trading life.

The place was more solidly anti-Jacobite than any other important Scots town. The Prince's army might very easily have sacked it, for it was quite unprotected, its own volunteers having been withdrawn to protect Edinburgh. But Provost Cochrane dealt cannily and also courageously with the Jacobite requisitions. Prince Charles's retreating army marched into Glasgow on Christmas Day, 1745, and the Prince established himself in the Shawfield Mansion. Dougal Graham, the hunchbacked pedlar who became the city's bellman and the least inhibited writer of popular stories in Scots whom Glasgow has known, describes the Highlanders' entry in lively doggerel.

> The shot was rusted in the gun,
> Their swords from scabbards would not twin,
> Their count'nance fierce as a wild bear,
> Out o'er their eyes hung down their hair,
> Their very thighs red tanned quite,
> But yet as nimble as they'd been white.
> Some of them did barefooted run
> Minded no mire or stoney groun;
> But when shaven, drest and clothed again
> They turned to be like other men.

They were, in fact, re-clothed at the town's expense. The Prince held court for a week among uncertain or unfriendly faces. Probably he met again the Glasgow girl, Clementina Walkinshaw of Barrowfield, who was his mother's godchild and was to be his mistress in exile. He reviewed his troops on the Green. And then he marched away again to win his last victory at Falkirk, where two regiments of Glasgow volunteers on the Hanoverian side suffered severely. These casualties and the levy of £14,000 (most of it repaid by the Government) were all that the city suffered in this last war of the Stewarts who had been its neighbours and sovereigns, almost its sons.

This story brings out the extraordinary isolation of the town, and the independence that went with it. Glasgow was nearer to being a city republic after the Union than it had been when the centre of government was in Edinburgh. The Scots capital had been only a long day's journey away. Till very nearly the end of the eighteenth century, an exchange of letters with London took almost a fortnight. Though it was usually very careful to keep on the right side of the law, the Town Council had to take decisions which would make any modern bailie blanch. It subsidised new ventures. It raised and armed a police force. It could, and did, incorporate all sorts of bodies, from trade unions to commercial companies and cultural associations, even a university. Typically enough, five years after the Prince's visit it granted a seal of cause (the incorporating privilege) to a Highland Society, whose main object was the apprenticing of poor boys from the north to trades in the city—this was very much in the spirit of Bailie Nicol Jarvie.

The prospering city began to feel after other fine things besides learning. Architecture is the art that has flourished most constantly in Glasgow itself, but the first Glasgow artists to make an impression on the outer world were two printers, Robert and Andrew Foulis. It is reasonable to talk of fine art where their work is concerned. They had prepared themselves for it by careful study, at home, in England and on the Continent. They were able to use remarkably fine types produced by Alexander Wilson, a man of varied skills who became Glasgow University's first Professor of Astronomy. With the encouragement of the University, the Foulis brothers produced a whole series of splendidly printed books in Greek, Latin and English—the most famous of them being a Homer in four folio volumes. The whole enterprise, in a town which had no tradition of fine printing, was an astonishing thing, very typical of one side of the Glasgow character, which has so often refused to recognise material obstacles when it has been seised of a pleasing and promising idea.

73

When his printing had begun to prove its merits, Robert Foulis immersed himself in a yet more adventurous scheme, and one which, since its success depended on others besides himself and his brother, proved, not surprisingly, to be less fortunate. He had visited some of the great continental schools of art, and saw no reason why Glasgow (which had produced scarcely a painter or sculptor of its own) should not begin to do as well as Paris.* He got the support of the University, which lent him rooms, and of three eminent merchants, who were prepared to finance an Academy of Arts in Glasgow. For twenty years the effort continued. It produced one or two respectable painters and the medallion maker, James Tassie, whose portraits in paste have scarcely been surpassed. Its annual shows were certainly discussed: to the end some Glaswegians seem to have found their existence a little perplexing. Quite probably the plan of the London Royal Academy was influenced by Foulis's example. But in 1775, the enterprise collapsed. The brothers died, leaving nothing but debt and their magnificent books behind them. It was nearly a century before painting, as an art, really found its place in Glasgow.

The merchant city has left one noble relic in stone. St. Andrew's Church, off the Saltmarket, was begun in 1739 and was seventeen years building. This leisurely progress certainly suggests that the town councillors' attitude to such work had changed—that their interest was in the production of a fine monument to the city's wealth and taste quite as much as in giving the steadily swelling population a new place of worship. The design, by a Glasgow architect, Allan Dreghorn, is said to be based on that of St. Martin-in-the-Fields. The resemblance of the Glasgow church to the London one is not, however, very close. Standing in the wreck of what, a few years since, was a seemly square, St. Andrew's still has elegance. The urns above its walls are too insistent, but it has a really fine western portico, and the interior, with its Corinthian columns, rococo decoration and crowned mahogany pulpit has no parallel in Scotland. Close

* Robert Foulis had, however, a commercial object, that of making industrial designers. He "wished to see the manufacturers of our own country enjoying" the advantages of experience in "Drawing and Modelling".

16, 17 St. Andrew's Church
(mid-eighteenth century)
Allan Dreghorn, architect

18 The Old Bridge, looking to the Merchants House Steeple
From a drawing by John Fleming engraved by Joseph Swan in "Select Views of Glasgow", 1828

by is the little Episcopal church of St. Andrews-by-the-Green, carrying on its galleries the names of noble families who had attached themselves to this fashionable, though now dissenting, communion.

The most important work of the eighteenth century that remains to us, however, is the waterway of the River Clyde itself. "The Clyde made Glasgow, and Glasgow made the Clyde" is an old saying: the second statement is truer than the first. While the trading city was building itself up, the river was still quite incapable of carrying its ships, which had to sail from Port Glasgow or Greenock, more than 20 miles away. Till the seventeen-eighties, or even later, it was rare to see the masts of a square-rigged ship at the town's quay. The boats which used it were still lighters or gabbarts to which the goods landed at the mouth of the Firth had to be transferred. Plans for deepening the channel were continually being discussed, but it was not until 1773 that operations directed by John Golborne, of Chester, were seriously begun. At that time there were only 15 inches of water at low tide within 400 yards of Glasgow Bridge.* By dredging and the building of jetties to contract the channel, he brought the depth to over six feet. But the deepening process had to be carried a good deal further before ocean-going ships could reach Glasgow with ease. The Clyde remains an artificial waterway whose busy narrowness amazes strangers. By 1777, indeed, Glasgow was almost as effectively linked by water to the North Sea as to the Atlantic, for a new canal from the Forth at Grangemouth had reached Hamilton Hill, just north of the city. It did not become effectively a Forth-and-Clyde canal until 1790, when it was carried to the lower river at Bowling.

By this time, however, the first great age of merchant Glasgow was past. Tobacco imports had soared for half a century. In 1771 the Clyde imported 46,000,000 lb., and of this only 3,000,000 remained in Great Britain. The largest share of the rest went to France. The tobacco business accounted for by far the greater

---

* The new Glasgow Bridge, built in 1768 at what was then the extreme west end of the city. Glasgow people still prefer to call its successor on the same site "the Jamaica Bridge". The medieval bridge, reconstructed, lasted till 1847 and was then replaced.

part of the entire foreign trade of Scotland. The total imports of the country amounted to £1,386,329, re-exports (nearly all tobacco) were £1,353,841, and home produced exports £503,473.

The Tobacco Lords, the great merchants of the trade, dominated the Glasgow scene. Wearing scarlet cloaks and carrying gold-headed canes, they walked the Plainstanes, the one stretch of paving in the city, outside the new Exchange at the Cross, while lesser traders waited respectfully for a chance to speak with them. Their new, fine homes lay west of the older streets—one of them, the admired house of William Cunninghame of Lainshaw, still stands half-hidden behind the portico of the Stirling Library in Royal Exchange Square. Cunninghame was one of four men who did most to develop the tobacco trade and the industries and banks that went with it. Three of them lived to see it fall.

In 1775, the American colonies revolted. Supplies of tobacco were soon cut off at the source. Long before the war ended, nearly eight years later, hope for a full revival of Glasgow's tobacco trade was ended, since it became clear that, even if the colonists submitted, the main restriction on their commerce, which prevented them from dealing directly with the European continent, would have to be abandoned.

At first the Tobacco Lords and Glasgow magistrates showed a striking military spirit. They determined to raise a Glasgow regiment for the campaign and succeeded, at the cost of £10,000 and some personal exertion, for these usually unapproachable and magnificent persons were ready to head an impressive recruiting party. One beat a drum, another played the bagpipes, some acted as fifers or carried swords and colours. An ex-Lord Provost was in command.

Tobacco ships were used as transports. But the war went badly. The industries which had been built up to supply the colonies were in confusion. Most of the greater tobacco lords were able to retire to their country estates. Cunninghame of Lainshaw made a great new fortune by buying up the existing stocks of tobacco and holding them for the enormous rise in price that scarcity soon produced. But there were disastrous failures, especially where money had been put into American land, which was confiscated. For the first time in the century, there was serious unemployment. In 1782, the crops failed, and Glasgow was threatened with famine. A public spirited minister, Dr. Porteous, who had taken on the task of supervising poor relief found that one of his chief functions was to prevent strangers from the equally depressed shires round Glasgow from pouring into the city. They called him "Buff the Beggars". For a year or two, it looked as if the age of Glasgow's prosperity was ended for ever. And it still stood remote on the edge of its world.

CHAPTER FIVE

Cotton and Steam

1780 to 1837

THE fourth Glasgow began with the beginning of the United States. There had been the settlement which was not yet a town; the little city of the bishops, created for and by the Church; the merchant burgh, which stretched its interests over half the world. Now Glasgow became, quite suddenly, what it has remained ever since, one of the great centres of the new industrial age. Its ports were still busy: they were to grow busier for generations. But it was no longer to live mainly by distant trade alone. Its concern was with making as much (or more) than with buying and selling: most even of its greatest merchants were to be manufacturers too.

Yet the new Glasgow was not, to begin with, the kind of place it has been for a century past—a big, smoky centre of heavy industries; of steel and shipbuilding and engineering. What saved it when the American Revolution cut away the privileged tobacco trade was cotton. Glasgow and the counties round it were just ready to make the finest cloths of their kind in the world.

They had the wealth and the skill. The tobacco trade had provided the first of these. The rich men who survived the American crisis had to find new uses for their money, new freights for their ships. The fine linens which had gone across the Atlantic to pay for tobacco and sugar had trained a race of weavers, and the technicians who bleached, dyed and printed the cloths. The weavers of Paisley and the Glasgow suburb of Anderston had worked with imported silk and cotton thread too, but they could not equal Indian cotton until new means of spinning a really fine thread in Scotland were found. The inventions of Arkwright and Crompton in England filled this gap just before

19 Hutcheson's Hospital, Ingram Street (*David Hamilton, architect*; *about 1805*). The figures of the founders, George and Thomas Hutcheson, are of the seventeenth century

20 Carlton Place (*Peter Nicolson, architect*) and Gorbals Parish Church (*David Hamilton, architect*) with
the second Glasgow Bridge

From Swan's "Select Views of Glasgow", 1828

or during the American War. James Monteith, of Anderston, grandson of a Perthshire bonnet laird who had come to Glasgow to escape Rob Roy's depredations, produced a web of muslin so fine that it would pass through a ring. In his triumph, he had a dress made of it, embroidered with gold, which he presented to the Queen.

Here was Glasgow's chance. It was taken with remarkable speed by a group of able and enterprising men. The best remembered among them is David Dale, whose character is sometimes said to have given Scott the idea of his Bailie Nicol Jarvie, though Dale had no romantic link with any Highland chieftain. In half a dozen ways, however, he was certainly a type of the immensely active Glasgow men who seized their place in the new world of industry.

"I fell all my length on the ice," exclaimed David, one winter's day. "Be thankful it was not all your breadth," said an unfeeling friend. Glasgow often smiled at David Dale, and he returned the smile. But he was highly respected—with reason. When the eminent Lord Provost Patrick Colquhoun boldly founded the first British Chamber of Commerce for a Glasgow anxiously seeking new business in 1783, David Dale was vice-president, though he had no claim to be a member of the almost hereditary merchant patriciate and his greatest achievements were just beginning.

He had been a weaver. Then he began to do a little business in linen yarn, tramping round farms and cottages to buy it from domestic spinners. Next he set up business (in half of a shop near the Cross) as an importer of yarns from the Continent. He became a tape manufacturer and a maker of printed cloth. All these things led him towards cotton. In 1783, when he was forty-four, his enterprise suddenly blossomed in three directions. He took over the other half of the shop at Glasgow Cross (rent £2 10s.) and established there the first successful Glasgow branch of one of the great Edinburgh banks, the Royal, with himself as agent. With an ingenious Highlander, George Macintosh, he founded the first turkey-red work in Great Britain, producing dyes suitable for cotton. And he began negotiations with Richard Arkwright, the Lancashire inventor, which led to the opening of the first great cotton mill, at New Lanark, three years later.

New Lanark is a historic name. Like the other cotton mills that fed the first industrial Glasgow, it was built to use water power: in this case from the Falls of Clyde. Like most of them (for this reason) it does not lie close to the city. But unlike most of them it still exists—the fast-flowing streams of Renfrewshire, Lanarkshire and other western counties are set with the ruins or the transformed remains of such mills. Unlike most of these others, too, New Lanark was not only a commercial success but a social experiment. David Dale was a man with a conscience; a pattern not only of business acumen but of something less common, but characteristic of the Glasgow that followed him, practical philanthropy. Many of his employees were orphan children, the pathetic little serfs of the early factories. Dale supplied them with carefully regulated food, accommodation, and schooling—and also with sweets when he came out to the mill.★ He built houses for his workers, remarkably good for his day, and was continually planning for their welfare.

When Robert Owen, the socialist prophet, married his daughter and took over the mill, much more ambitious reforms were introduced and New Lanark became a show place for inquiring visitors, including a future Tsar. But Owen built on David Dale's foundations, moral as well as material. Dale was constantly thinking for and spending on other people. With his friend Mackintosh he set up cotton mills in the Highlands, near Dornoch and Oban, with the idea of giving employment rather than of making profit: they were no more successful than other attempts to put large factories into a country not made for such things, but the experiment, in his day, was at least a new one. In the first bad years of depression and threatened famine which struck industrial Glasgow, he chartered ships to bring in grain for the poor.

He gave as much time and energy to religion as to all his half-

★ They worked 13 hours a day and slept three in a bed, but there is no reason to doubt that their health and comfort were far above the average of the time.

dozen businesses. There, too, he was an original. He helped to found a sect "the Old Scotch Independents", preached Sunday by Sunday to a Glasgow congregation and, to master this work, taught himself Greek and Hebrew. For a while he was hooted at in the streets and mobs attacked his chapel, but all that was soon forgotten, and his pastorate continued for 37 years. There was nothing narrowly puritanical about his way of life. He built himself a handsome home to Robert Adam's design in Charlotte Street beside the Green. When he was about to give an important dinner party, floods from the Clyde and the Molendinar invaded his cellars and kitchen. But neighbouring kitchens were mobilised to meet the crisis. His daughter, who was to be Owen's bride, was carried to the cellar on a porter's back and brought out the wine. It was reckoned to have been an unusually cheerful and satisfying occasion.

Charlotte Street was one of the pleasantest places in the new Glasgow. Its fate is typical of what has happened to many of them. Twenty years ago, the façades of a series of villas in the Adam style could at least hint at the first suburban beauty of its wide lower reach, while some remarkably handsome, though dilapidated, Georgian tenements looked down on them from the north. There are still a few battered remnants, but nearly everything is gone, including David Dale's own house, which was unlucky enough to fall into the hands of the city's Education Committee, who felt that its site might make a school playground.

The Glasgow of the age of cotton must, indeed, have been a strikingly handsome place. In its earliest years it certainly roused the enthusiasm of one observer, John Mayne.

> Wow, sirs! it's wonderfu' to trace
> How commerce has improved the place,
> Changing bare house-room's narrow space,
>   And want o' money,
> To seats of elegance and grace,
>   And milk and honey.
>
> In ilka house, frae man to boy,
> A' hands in Glasgow find employ;

Even little maids, wi' meikle joy,
  Flower lawn and gauze,
Or clip wi' care the silken soy
  For ladies's braws.

Their faithers weave, their mothers spin
The muslin robe, so fine and thin
That frae the ankle to the chin,
  In aft discloses
The beauteous symmetry within—
  Limbs, necks and bosies.

Tween twa' and three, wi' daily care,
The gentry to the Cross repair
The Politician, wi' grave air,
  Deliberating,
Merchants and manufact'rers there
  Negotiating

Look through the town! The houses here
Like noble palaces appear;
A' things the face o' gladness wear—
  The market's thrang,
Business is brisk, and a's asteer
  The streets alang.

Wondering, we see new streets extending,
New squares wi' public buildings blending,
Brigs, stately brigs, in arches bending
  Across the Clyde,
And turrets, kirks, and spires ascending
  In lofty pride.

The town was constantly and rapidly growing, with 67,000 people in 1791 and 202,000 forty years later. It was no longer "the beautifullest little city" of a century earlier. It was, in fact, the second city of the British Empire. The old streets remained, though they were becoming too closely packed, "improvement" had done away with most of the famous piazzas, and the gardens were being built upon. There was still a hint of green leaves about some of them, however. And the new streets which were constantly spreading, particularly to the west and south of the river, had a style of their own. It was, in the main, a classical style, strongly influenced by memories of the Adams. Several of the Adam buildings themselves are lost now—not only David Dale's house, but the first Royal Infirmary beside the cathedral (replaced by a vast block only very faintly reminiscent of its beginnings) and the Assembly Rooms (on the site of the present central Post Office) which have left one surprising fragment, a Roman archway transported to the Green. But Robert Adam's Trades House, built in 1794 to give the city guilds a home worthy of their wealth and dignity still remains in Glassford Street. It is a little dwarfed by the tall insignificance of its neighbours to the south, but its strong façade and cupola express its owners' not extravagant self-confidence with dignity.

This was the most notable public building in Glasgow's first New Town, a place of wide streets and squares planned when the New Town of Edinburgh had set a standard for Scotland. It is very much broken up now by Victorian and later intrusions. One finely planned public place remains—Royal Exchange Square, with its entrance arches from Buchanan Street, and, in the centre, David Hamilton's high-windowed, temple-like Exchange. Preserved by a Town Council which, in this case has shown a real architectural conscience, it now houses the Stirling Library. But in their day the long lines of tenements and terraces, gleaming in cream-coloured stone, must have been more impressive than any single building as they spread westward from the old centre of the city, climbing the hill towards Blythswood Square. Facing the river from the south, Carlton Place, with its aristocratic-looking church (also by David Hamilton, but now much tattered) had a rich, palatial air, and some of the streets behind it are still impressive, though their social prosperity is long since gone.

The Glasgow of this time was still scarcely stained by smoke. In the 'twenties and 'thirties, high chimneys had begun to colour the sunset, but steam-driven factories were few so long as cotton depended on water-power for spinning, and on the work of weavers, who wrought in their own homes. The beginning of the nineteenth century was the great age of the weavers. "Then", wrote one of them, "was the daisy portion of weaving, the bright and midday period of all who pitched a shuttle and of the happy one whose luck it was to win a weaver's smile." A skilled craftsman could earn the enormous sum of £2 per week—as much as a professional man outside the cities. On Sundays the weaver would appear with powdered hair, a gold-headed cane, and falls of linen at the sleeves of his blue coat, while his wife walked beside him in her red cloak.

Throughout its existence, the Scottish cotton trade concentrated on fine cloth. This was the source of the workers' prosperity to begin with, as well as of the manufacturers' and merchants'. But when mechanical weaving became possible and steam power drew the mills into the city, the craftsman's sky darkened, economically as well as physically. His skill became a snare. Because he could work so finely he could compete with the machines for a generation or more. But they wore him down. His earnings could fall to 8s. a week, or less. And because his cloths were made for the richest markets, each change of fashion was apt to throw him out of work for a while. The social problems of its new industries began to press on Glasgow even where the most intelligent and highly trained of its workers were concerned.

The years that were the weaver's "daisy portion" were prosperous and optimistic for most other people. Through many of them, to be sure, there was war. Glasgow sent thousands of recruits to the armies that fought the French Revolution and Napoleon, among them the greatest soldier it has bred, John Moore. He was born just west of the Cross, the great-grandson of the provost who brought Glasgow successfully through the Whig Revolution of 1689. Sir John Moore's victories and his death at Corunna no doubt excited and saddened his fellow citizens. They had cheerful memories of his father (also John Moore) a famous social character, doctor and novelist, before he left Glasgow for London.

On the whole, however, the French wars did not weigh too heavily, at any rate during most of their course. There

were alarms and crises and the drilling of volunteers. But the
Atlantic trade grew, and suffered little. For the middle and
directing classes, life was becoming more varied. After much
discouragement, since most Presbyterians were convinced that
it was the Devil's house, the theatre was establishing itself.
There were weekly dances in the new Assembly Rooms. Concerts were organised which attracted "the best performers".
Middle-class Glasgow was still (as almost all Glasgow had been
since the time of the first merchants) a town of flats. But the
more prosperous no longer concealed beds in their living rooms.
There were dinner parties of many courses, and polite tea-
drinking:

> They chat of dress (as ladies will), of cards,
> And fifty friends within three hundred yards,
> Or now they listen, all in merry glee,
> While "Nancy Dawson", "Sandie o'er the lea"
> (Than foreign music truly sweeter far)
> Ring on the jingling spinet or guitar.
> The clogs are ready, when the meal is o'er,
> And many a blazing lantern leaves the door.

For the men there was a much heavier and longer continued kind
of drinking in houses or (much oftener) in taverns. The careful
frugality that had once governed most meetings of that sort was
gone. It no longer thought necessary to be home by ten o'clock.
There were strange frolics in the streets, assaults on the usually
aged guardians of the peace, a Hell-fire Club, one of whose
drunken pranks destroyed the old Tron Kirk, a thunderous
moment when barrels full of stones were sent rolling down the
slope towards the midnight Trongate. For a while the Kirk itself
seemed to lose some of its hold over these hereditary Presbyterians. It was in dissenting chapels, like David Dale's, that
religion seemed most alive, and the number of these was
constantly increasing.

Later the war touched Glasgow rather more closely. The ablest
Glasgow merchant of his time, Kirkman Finlay (who was also a
great cotton spinner) set himself to break through the Continental System which Napoleon established to exclude British

exports from Europe. He organised underground agencies on the Continent and depots at Heligoland and elsewhere just beyond the limits of Napoleon's power, from which the blockade could be run. Later he invaded the monopoly of the East India Company and sent the first Glasgow ship to Calcutta.

No figure in Glasgow life was so powerful and, for a time, so popular. He had all the honours that the town and University could give him. In 1812, while he was still Lord Provost, he was elected M.P. for the Glasgow Burghs. Medals were struck. Enthusiasts of the highest respectability drew him in his carriage from the Cross to his house in Queen Street. At this point the darker side of the times began to appear. The cost of the war was mounting. Weavers' earnings began to fall disastrously. There were strikes in that and other trades. The next time excited citizens surrounded Finlay's house, they went to smash its windows. This was in March, 1815. He had been voting for the Corn Bill, which would raise or maintain the high price of bread.

The war had begun among political alarms of a sort long unfamiliar to Glasgow people. The eighteenth-century spirit of the place had been, on the whole, a liberal one. Revered professors toasted the fall of the Bastille. But as the French Revolution developed the alarm of established authorities in Britain grew with it. The idea of political reform at home, long familiar and respectable enough, was treated as sedition. It chilled town councillors as well as M.P.s, for if taxpayers were allowed to vote for a new Parliament, they would surely expect to elect their councils too. Thomas Muir of Huntershill, the son of a Glasgow merchant, was the first Scottish martyr of reform. He was an eloquent, courageous and high-principled young man who had become an advocate in Edinburgh, an eager organiser of political societies and meetings, and also an elder of the Kirk. The story of his arrest, his journey to France to plead for the life of King Louis, his return after war had been declared, his shameful trial*—in which, however, Glasgow men like David Dale

* It was on this occasion that Lord Braxfield, the presiding judge, welcomed a juryman with the whisper, "Come awa', Maister Horner, and help us to hang ane o' thae damned scoondrels."

21 Glasgow from the Green in the 1820's
From Swan's "Select Views of Glasgow", 1828

22   The Trades House, Glassford Street
William Adam, architect

23   Glasgow of the 1820's: the eastern block of Blythswood Square,
now the Royal Scottish Automobile Club

conspicuously refused to support his prosecutors—his transportation to Australia, his rescue by the Americans, his escape after a British attack on the ship that was carrying him to Europe again, Napoleon's intervention to save him, and his death near Paris from wounds received in the naval fight—all this is an almost unbelievable piece of tragic romance.

After Muir's day, however, political agitation in Scotland, which had never threatened serious violence, died away. As the war was ending it began to revive again. Once more the Government smelt revolution. The rulers of Glasgow had become more and more deeply steeped in Toryism—not the old Toryism of the Jacobites, but the new Toryism of wealth and the heirs of Mr. Pitt. According to one story, when Kirkman Finlay was asked to present a Reform petition in Parliament on behalf of the unenfranchised, he replied by demanding whether there was not, in Scotland, a widespread, secret conspiracy to overthrow the Government. The story is doubtful because it comes to us from Alexander Richmond, once a leader of the weavers, who was afterwards denounced as a spy and *agent provocateur*.

It is charitable to assume that Finlay and the ministers in London with whom he dealt believed that a serious conspiracy really existed. Perhaps there was such a thing, though there is very little evidence for it in Scotland, except what Richmond himself provided. The weavers were certainly a reading and arguing race. A man could talk with his friends, and sometimes even scan a book, as he sat at his loom. They were apt to be Radicals in politics, just as they were apt to belong to dissenting sects rather than to the established Church. But when, in 1817, Richmond supplied Finlay with copies of an "indissoluble bond" signed by a dozen weavers, who demanded manhood suffrage and annual Parliaments and swore to support the programme "either by moral or physical force", there seems to be little doubt that he had composed the document himself. It was produced in the House of Commons. Though a prosecution based on it collapsed scandalously the legend of Red Glasgow had been born.

It has lasted till our own day, and it was soon to be carried a great deal further. In 1820 discontent was rising higher than ever. The most extraordinary rumours began to circulate in Scotland, and even to appear in the newspapers. The English Radicals were rising—they had marched into Scotland and seized the Carron Ironworks—5,000 revolutionary Frenchmen were about to appear on Cathkin Braes, where Glasgow now has a park.

On 1st April, a proclamation of "the Committee for forming a Provisional Government" appeared on Glasgow walls calling the people to arms. It appears that this was Richmond's work. There were strikes. The factories were closed. Glasgow's streets were full of idle men. The city was far more heavily garrisoned than it had ever been in the warlike crises of the past. Through a day and night of storm and lashing rain, its volunteer Sharpshooters stood to their arms,* and cannon commanded the bridges. A handful of workmen did answer the spurious call. Almost twenty marched on Glasgow from the weaving village of Strathaven, but turned back when they found no rally at Cathkin. Thirty of a group who had started their march from Glasgow actually faced a charge of hussars near Falkirk. There were many arrests. A prosecutor was sent from England to apply the treason law which had been imposed on Scotland after the Union. James Wilson of Strathaven (called Perley, because he was said to have invented the pearl stitch) was hanged and beheaded at Glasgow Green. Andrew Hardie and John Baird suffered at Stirling. All three were weavers: Hardie was an ancestor of Keir Hardie, founder of the Scottish Labour Party. The Government had made its example. The "Radical War" was over: this miserable little eruption of cultivated fears and delusions was all the revolution that Glasgow has ever seen.

There were others who took a rather more constructive view of social problems than Kirkman Finlay and his associates. In the past, poverty of a really harrowing sort had been regarded as an exceptional thing, to be met with exceptional efforts like David Dale's. Now industry was drawing in streams of country people who had no experience of town life and no resources of their

---

* They were commanded by Samuel Hunter, a cheerful and respected journalist, who first made *The Glasgow Herald* the city's representative newspaper.

own to carry them through years of depression. Slums were beginning to appear. They were not quite so bad in the first quarter of the new century as they were to become soon afterwards, when Irish and Highlanders from turf cabins and "black houses" were packed more and more closely into the old wynds of the city. But conditions were already shocking enough. The first serious attempt to deal with them was made by one of the most remarkable men in the city's history, Thomas Chalmers, whose influence on Glasgow's way of thinking was almost as deep as Adam Smith's had been.

This pale-eyed, pale-haired minister with awkward gestures and a strong Fife accent was an orator of extraordinary power. When he preached in London he drew tears from Cabinet ministers. In post-war Glasgow he packed the Tron Kirk and electrified a generation which was already inclined to be more serious-minded than the men of 1800. He spoke and wrote about economics, about astronomy, about the organisation of the Church—all these things were linked to his evangelism. His ideas on social questions were as far from those of our day as they could be. Though he was (on the whole) a Conservative in politics, he had the deepest distrust of the State's powers—in the end he was to tear the Church of Scotland in two rather than accept the decisions of Governments which had no understanding of Scottish Presbyterianism. He was horrified by the pauperisation which wholesale grants of parish relief had produced in England, and he had a plan for Glasgow: in effect he aimed at dealing with poverty by private enterprise.

He got himself transferred to a new parish, of 10,000 people —St. John's. It was the most depressed in the city, but he undertook that his church would deal with its poor, financing the work from part of the Sunday collections. He appointed twenty-five deacons, each of whom had a district of his own. These men were to study each case of poverty, to try to find work for the distressed, or friends or relatives who would help them, before they gave relief. Under Chalmers, the system seemed to work. But it was strongly opposed. Other parishes in the city and out of it refused to adopt his programme. He left St. John's for a

professorship, and in 1837 the experiment he had started was
abandoned. To the end, he was convinced that he had shown
Scotland the proper way of dealing with its poor.

"If England," he wrote, "will so idolise her own institutions
as be unwilling to part with even the most vicious she must be
let alone, since she will have it so. But let her not inoculate
with the virus of her own gangrene those countries which have
the misfortune to border on her territory and be subject to her
sway; and, more especially, let not the simple and venerated
parochial system of our land lie open to the crudities, or be placed
at the disposal of a few cockney legislators."★

Chalmers was, perhaps, almost too anxious to insist on the
economic value of his plans, to prove that they saved money.
This obscured his driving idea, that even in a great industrial city
the personal efforts of Christian men should be able to deal with
all human problems. Perhaps it was an impossible idea, though a
magnificent one. Certainly Glasgow failed to apply it fully. But
it left its imprint on the minds of Glasgow men for the best part
of a century.

Meanwhile, the industrial age was showing a new face. Steam
was coming in. More than two years before Chalmers came to the
Tron, the first trail of smoke was seen on the Clyde. Before he
left, little steamers were darting everywhere about the Firth and
out to Belfast, Liverpool and even London. Ships and engines
were being built for England and other countries.

Steam, as the motive power that really kept nineteenth-
century industry going, had, in a sense, its beginnings in Glasgow.
It was in a corner of the old University buildings that James Watt
worked on the models and plans which produced the first
generally useful steam-engine. He was there because, not being
a member of one of the town's chartered trade incorporations,
he could not practise outside the privileged limits of the College.
It was, when he was walking on Glasgow Green in 1764 that he
had the crowning idea of a separate condenser, which made his
engine a practicable thing. But though his great work began in
Glasgow it was in Birmingham that he built and developed his

★ *On the Sufficiency of the Parochial System Without a Poor Rate*, p. 140.

24 The New Town in the 1820's: George Square. A carriage is leaving the site of the present City Chambers

From Swan's "Select Views of Glasgow", 1828

25 Glasgow Harbour, looking towards the Broomielaw. An early river steamer is on the left
From Swan's "Select Views of Glasgow", 1828

engines. Steam power came slowly into Glasgow's cotton mills. By 1800 there were only eight steam engines in the Scottish cotton business—the industry lived by water power. Thirty years later the great change had arrived: there were 107 steam-driven mills in Glasgow and its suburbs.

But long before that steam power had transformed Glasgow's trade and given it what were really two new industries. The first Scottish steamer—it is doubtful if it can be called the first in the world—was a tiny pleasure boat on which the poet Burns sailed round Dalswinton Loch in Dumfriesshire in 1788. The designer of its engine was William Symington, of Leadhills. Fourteen years later, the first commercially practicable steam-boat appeared on the Forth and Clyde Canal: its use was forbidden lest it should wash away the canal banks. Then, in 1812, the *Comet* was launched on the Clyde. It was a little paddle boat, only 38 feet long and so shallow that when it stuck on a sandbank in the still badly dredged river on its first voyage, its crew stepped overboard and pushed it off again. Henry Bell, its inventor and owner, made little by his enterprise. But as soon as its practical success was known new steamers appeared.

At last Glasgow's natural disadvantages as a port were properly overcome. Steamboats, or ships controlled by steam tugs, could face the journey up and down the river at any state of the wind and tide. The further deepening of the Clyde was really worth while, and it went ahead steadily. Shipbuilding went ahead too. It was not an old Glasgow trade: in the sixteenth century special encouragement was given to a boat-builder because he was the only man of his craft in the city. Sea-going ships were built at Greenock for the Glasgow merchants, but in the days of the Tobacco Lords most were bought from America. It was the coming of steamships which, by degrees, concentrated the industry in the Clyde and first attracted it to the city itself.

This, too, was the real beginning of Glasgow engineering. The Napiers, David and Robert, were soon the greatest designers of marine engines in the world. A new craftsmanship was born. It soon spread into other types of engine-making. Steam was now taking to rails. Glasgow got a steam railway of its own in 1831, when the Garnkirk line was opened. Almost from the first, Glasgow built its engines for itself. But the real age of railway travel did not dawn till Victoria was Queen.

By that time the city had a new form of government. The Tories had at last lost power in Parliament, and the Reformers (moderate-minded reformers) had come in. On the whole, Glasgow opinion was on their side. Until the nineteenth century, the old style of town council, representing only the Merchants and the Incorporated Trades, had worked pretty well. Many of the lord provosts and magistrates were remarkable men. But the system had begun to break down. People were unwilling to pay rates to an authority which they did not choose, and when a proper police force was seen to be absolutely necessary, elected commissioners were set up to control it.★ Political excitement was concentrated mainly on the reform of Parliament. Even the privileged Trades House was behind it. Glasgow was to have two M.P.s of its own, chosen by taxpayers and not by the Town Council. When the Bill that promised this as well as so many other changes was held up, 10,000 protesters gathered on Glasgow Green. When it was passed, the city blazed with gas jets of joy. The change in Parliament was soon followed by burgh reform. The old closed council was swept away—its only vestige in 1956 is the presence in the elected Corporation of the Dean of Guild (head of the Merchants House) and the Deacon Convener of the Trades. Refreshed politically, still growing, still finding new ways to wealth (and new poor), still on the edge of its world, Glasgow was ready for the Victorian Age.

★ The Glasgow Council's first independent experiment in this direction had failed.

CHAPTER SIX

The Age of Grey Ashlar

1837 to 1880

IN spite of the centuries that lie behind it, Glasgow, the stone and lime that we know—is a Victorian city. You might almost call it *the* Victorian city, the one great town which has maintained a nineteenth-century face of which it may be reasonably proud. Architecturally, the Victorian Age was not a great period. Though we are beginning to appreciate what was good in it much more fully than the last generation could, it is never likely to rank with the supreme ages of building, if only because it was too anxious to imitate an enormous range of past styles. But it does not seem unreasonable to boast that Glasgow has the best, or very nearly the best, of what it could give, and that the Victorian best, in such quantity, is impressive.

No doubt it could be argued that Glasgow's Victorian streets are good to look at partly because comparatively few of their buildings are wholly in the Victorian taste. Scottish builders have often been behind the reigning fashion, and, occasionally, in advance of it. There are things of the late Middle Ages which look almost pre-Gothic. On the other hand, several of the architects who brought neo-classicism to London were Scots. In the middle of Queen Victoria's reign, Glasgow men were still continuing or developing a sort of work which England might think Georgian. Sir John James Burnet (1859–1938) even carried this tradition on beyond the end of the century, and took its latest fruits back to London, after C. R. Mackintosh, in Glasgow itself, had leapt far into the twentieth century. Perhaps it is worth noticing that Burnet, one of the few Glasgow architects who had their training outside Scotland, was a student at the École des Beaux Arts in Paris. Yet even the most classical of the

Glasgow Victorians were, after all Victorians still. They were building good things for one of the great ages of human history.

At the end of Queen Victoria's reign, the population (including that of the suburbs which are now part of the city) was four times as large as it had been at the beginning. It was more than a million. Almost all these people were housed and worked in tall sandstone buildings. The material controlled the shape and look of the place. The extravagances and irrelevancies of Victorian taste were repressed or became more seemly when they had to grow out of rock, instead of being moulded in brick or plaster. The insignificance of little houses, perhaps homely, but degenerating into a featureless desert when they are massed together, was scarcely known in nineteenth-century Glasgow, which sometimes ended in a fringe of stone villas, set in their gardens, but was often as sharply defined as a walled town, with four-storey tenements rising from the edge of the fields.

The Glasgow we know has a great core of grey, a pink fringe, and a wide frill of brick disguised by harling. The grey stone is mostly early- or mid-Victorian. It came from quarries in or about the town itself. Cleaned, most of it shows a warm cream colour. "Grey Glasgow" must have glowed when it was built. The red stone of the fringe—and of some buildings in the main commercial streets—belongs to the years between the late eighteen-eighties and 1914. It was brought from Dumfriesshire, Ayrshire, and Arran when the local quarries began to fail. The brick of the housing schemes came after the First German War.

Mainly Victorian as it is, grey Glasgow has a style, or at least a mixture of styles sufficiently similar to give some effect of decent and dignified uniformity. The pattern was set by the architects who came after the Adams. Their models, except for some churches, were classical and Renaissance, and they followed one another, forming a school that lasted throughout the nineteenth century, and has even outlived it.

If a Glasgow man mildly interested in such things was asked for a list of the chief architects who have worked there, he might name Robert Adam, David Hamilton, "Greek" Thomson, C. R. Mackintosh and Sir John James Burnet. All but one of these were

Glasgow men and only two did important work outside the west of Scotland. Adam was not a Glasgow architect in any sense—his name would be included because it is internationally famous. It is unlikely that our Glaswegian would be able to mention any other architect from the outer world whose building he recognised in the city, unless it were Sir George Gilbert Scott, who would be the subject not of praise but of a cautionary tale.

Victorian Glasgow swelled out from the Georgian New Town which, in the process, was partly transformed or destroyed. New quarters were planned as it grew. Sometimes the planning was fully carried out. Sometimes, in the hurry of that explosive age, it broke down or was abandoned. But most parts of Victorian Glasgow have a recognisable shape. Naturally enough, this is best seen where they are most spacious, in the streets that were built for the successful middle class.

There were, of course, many architects besides the five that an intelligent Glaswegian might name. Some of them worked from Edinburgh. Royal Exchange Square, with its arches from Buchanan Street, which makes a frame for David Hamilton's Exchange, is by Archibald Elliot. The two men's work makes a composition (pre-Victorian) that is one of the finest things in the city. It was Hamilton, however, who established the succession of Glasgow architects. Like some of those who followed him, he seems to have got his first training as a builder: like them, he obviously learned a great deal from books, but his practical knowledge of working with stone must have helped to guide him. Hamilton's pupil, Charles Wilson, a Glasgow builder's son, is perhaps the first of the true Victorians. When the city took a further step west in 1854, he and Sir Joseph Paxton (of the Crystal Palace*) were commissioned to lay out a new park, Kelvingrove. Wilson had the designing of the buildings crowning the hill of Woodlands which thrusts itself into the park.

This was municipal planning, and planning which suggests that there was good taste among the bailies. Fine terraces had already begun to climb westwards along the base and slope of the hill. They are rather reminiscent of the New Town of Edinburgh;

---

* Paxton also designed Queen's Park, to the south of the city.

one of their architects, in fact, was an Edinburgh man. Wilson's façades are in the towering buildings of Park Terrace which look out from the hilltop and still more notably, in Park Circus and its approaches, which are screened by the Terrace and Quadrant against the west winds. The outer buildings are dramatic enough; perhaps, with their mansard roofs and high, flattish bow windows, they are too much in the Victorian taste to please us completely. But Park Circus is a remarkable thing, a Roman piazza on a Scottish hilltop. Its balanced mass, its strong and simple decoration, make a lasting impression of magnificence. From the Terrace, a monumental stair to the level of the park surprises us. It, too, is Wilson's work. And to the east, below his Circus, he built what was then the Free Church College, with its twin towers, and its high-reaching, square campanile. Perhaps it was accident rather than design which matched with Wilson's work the contrasting but remarkably congruous tower of J. T. Rochead's Park Church. The "Park towers" form a notable group which catches the upward-glancing eye from several quarters of the city.

Buildings of the same sort of quality and dignity were rising in other parts of Victorian Glasgow—in the business centre and the Blythswood quarter, which had been part of the New Town, in Great Western Road and its neighbourhood, near the river at Finnieston. Charles Wilson was responsible for the fine central block of the High School in Elmbank Street (it was built to house the new Glasgow Academy) and for the much admired but more "correctly" imitative Italian hall of the Faculty of Procurators in St. George's Place.

The work of the best-remembered of Glasgow's Victorian architects overlaps Wilson's. Alexander Thomson came out of the Covenanting tradition. That is something to remember when one looks at the sphinx-like heads which support the tower of his best-known church in St. Vincent Street or recalls the clamouring colours of the interior of another, the one Glasgow building of interest destroyed by bombing. His religion had so little use for images in its worship that he could afford to indulge in fantastic forms and vaguely symbolic decorations.

The United Presbyterians, who commissioned his churches, were of the same tradition as himself. R. L. Stevenson wrote sarcastically of "the bonny U. P. Kirks", but, in Glasgow at least, some of the finest Victorian churches belonged to this denomination, now reunited with its parent national stem. Their architects had the advantage of knowing that what was wanted from them was not (necessarily) a longish building with a chancel, on the Gothic pattern, but simply a hall of any shape that a preacher could easily dominate. Internally, Thomson's St. Vincent Street church has rather the air of a theatre with its deep gallery. But it has a strangely exotic air, too. One can almost see the blind Samson laying his hands on one of those climbing pillars (cast-iron beneath the paint though they are) to bring down the Philistines about his head.

For, though his town knew its designer as "Greek" Thomson, memories of the Old Testament surely coloured his mind and work. Greece was, indeed, part of his inspiration, as it was that of so many Glasgow architects. Many of his Greek details and porticos are very fine, and he was apt, most ingeniously, to turn every many-windowed wall into a sort of colonnade. But he would borrow almost as readily from ancient Egyptian models as from Greek ones—Egyptian columns, pylon-like openings, lotus forms, even Greco-Egyptian chimney-pots. He did not wish to be an imitator, and his combination of these antique forms is surely original.

The St. Vincent Street church, growing out of a hillside, is wonderfully impressive from the south, but, in spite of its temple-like shape and porticos, it has very little of the Greek serenity. There is nervous force in his "Egyptian Halls", with their tremendous cornice scarcely noticed by to-day's Union Street crowds who seldom lift their eyes above the shop windows. There is even a curious sort of gaiety about the Grosvenor Restaurant façade in Gordon Street, which also has reminiscences of Egypt now stultified by an irrelevant Renaissance superstructure. Serenity does show itself in the finest of his domestic buildings, Great Western Terrace and Moray Place, and in the Caledonian Road Church—above all, in its square campanile, which has no classical original and scarcely a trace of Greek detail.

Thomson was not a fashionable architect, like Wilson. He belonged, essentially, to the south side of the town, rather than to the West End—for Londoners, that is rather like the contrast between Streatham and Belgravia—and he often had to build on awkward sites. He was not given the chance of designing any great public edifice. His one attempt to develop a group of streets in his own style probably broke down partly because, in those suburban regions, not yet officially part of the city, there was no one public authority to deal with it. His style was his own—its details were often imitated but its spirit was too original to be passed on. But his work typifies the spirit, the originality, the remoteness, too, from reigning fashions—of Victorian Glasgow, and one cannot doubt its influence in maintaining the classical traditions of building there.

Grey-stone Glasgow is not, of course, in the main, a place of terraces, churches and office buildings. It is a town of tenements —the usually four-storeyed blocks of flats in which most Glasgow people have lived for the best part of three centuries. High houses of this sort may have developed in Edinburgh partly because the area of the Old Town was restricted by nature and the needs of defence, but the style is a national one, no doubt influenced by Continental building habits—it was almost unknown in England. Some of the Glasgow tenements were individually designed by leading architects. Wilson's hand is seen in Garnethill and Greek Thomson's in Eglinton Street. But an almost universal pattern under which the ground floor might be used for shops, the first floor windows had ornamented cornices and the others were progressively plainer established itself. Bow windows break rather fussily through the lines of later buildings. There is no absolute uniformity, but the general effect is solidly handsome, if sometimes a little forbidding where the colour of the stone has ceased to kindle under the Western light.

There was, certainly, another side to this Victorian Glasgow. When the age began, or soon after that, the city had some of the worst slums in the world. On the old gardens behind the first

26   St. Vincent Street Church (1857–59)

Alexander Thomson, architect

27   Caledonia Road U.P. Church (1855), now Hutchesontown and
Caledonia Road Church
Alexander Thomson, architect

streets of the city, on narrower spaces behind parts of the eighteenth-century New Town, "backlands", cheap tenements had been pushed up to house thousands who came to look for work. The ancient houses of the wynds and closes★ were crammed with people—sometimes 300 shared one common stair with no sort of sanitation.

"The wynds of Glasgow", wrote an official commissioner, " comprise a fluctuating population of from 15,000 to 20,000 persons. This quarter consists of a labyrinth of lanes, out of which numberless entrances lead into small courts, each with a dunghill reeking in the centre. Revolting as was the outside of these places, I was little prepared for the filth and destitution within. In some of these lodging-rooms (visited at night) we found a whole lair of human beings littered along the floor—sometimes fifteen and twenty, some clothed, some naked—men, women and children huddled promiscuously together. Their bed consisted of a lair of rusty straw intermixed with rags. There was no furniture in these places. The sole article of comfort was a fire.

"A very extensive inspection of the lowest districts of other places, both here and on the Continent, never presented anything half so bad, either in intensity of pestilence, physical and moral, or in extent, proportional to the population."†

When the British Association met in Glasgow in 1840, the Chief Constable spoke to its members. "In the very centre of the city", he said, "there is an accumulated mass of squalid wretchedness, which is probably unequalled in the British Dominions. In the interior part of the square, bounded on the east by Saltmarket, on the west by Stockwell Street, on the North by Trongate, and on the south by the river, and also in certain parts of the east side of High Street . . . there is concentrated everything that is wretched, dissolute, loathsome and pestilential. These places are filled by a population of many thousands of miserable creatures. The houses are unfit even for styes, and

★ "Close" later came to mean not an enclosed piece of land but the entry to a tenement house.

† Commission on the Condition of Hand-loom Weavers Report, 1841.

every apartment is filled with a promiscuous crowd of men, women and children, all in the most revolting state of filth and squalor. In many of the houses there is scarcely any ventilation, and, from the extremely defective sewerage, filth of every kind constantly accumulates.''

In 1848, a year of revolutions throughout Europe, all this new misery boiled over into serious violence for the first and only time. There was trade depression and unemployment. Glasgow was crowded with refugees from the Irish and Highland potato famines.* Oatmeal was handed out to the starving. Great meetings were held on the Green. On 6th March, the mob that had gathered there marched on the city, crying "Vive la République". They sacked the foodshops, the gunsmiths, and the jewellers, and set up barricades round the Cross. Troops were brought up, and when, next day, an attack on one of the factories developed, there was firing in which six were killed. It was a far more serious business than the "Radical War", but this time there were no executions and the wave of discontent, which about the same time produced the abortive plan for a Chartist march on Parliament, died away.

The hero of this occasion was the Senior Bailie, Robert Stewart. The new elected Town Council still attracted successful business men. Stewart had already made a fortune as an ironmaster when he joined it at the age of thirty-two. Now, six years later, he found himself at the head of the city's affairs, for the Lord Provost, who was also an M.P., had to spend much of his time in London. When the cavalry faced the armed rioters, Robert Stewart rode beside their colonel. His influence did a great deal to calm the storm. Three years later, he was himself chosen Lord Provost and proceeded to win the city its first adequate water-supply.

More than a quarter of a million people depended either on ancient, contaminated wells, or on a private company which pumped water from the Clyde after the sewage of industrial

* Before 1795 there were possibly fewer than 100 Roman Catholics in Glasgow. By 1831 there were 26,000 and before the Famine perhaps 70,000, nearly all of them Irish or Highland. Today's Roman Catholic population is said to be above 300,000.

Lanarkshire had flowed into it. The Lord Provost proposed to draw on Loch Katrine, 34 miles away. The battle for this water is a famous Glasgow epic. The scheme was fiercely opposed. The Admiralty feared that the diversion of Loch Katrine water from the Forth would dry up its anchorages on the other side of Scotland. It was argued that the Loch was poisonous: it had, experts swore, a peculiar power of dissolving lead. Parliament threw out the Glasgow Bill in 1854, but next year it relented. Robert Stewart (now a mere councillor again) and his chief supporter in the fight, Bailie James Gourlay, had struck successfully against one of the chief carriers of disease.

But the Town Council still lacked power to attack the main roots of sickness and despair by dealing with the slums themselves, until it obtained a City Improvement Act in 1866. With this instrument, Glasgow began to cleanse itself, but it also destroyed its own past. "Backlands" were torn down, model tenements for re-housing were built in the suburbs, new streets were opened, old ones were widened and levelled. But what had been fine old houses in the High Street, Saltmarket, Gallowgate, and the picturesque old main street of the Gorbals, were also swept away. When railway companies wished to build lines through the old town they were welcomed as saviours. Their viaducts and bridges marched through the heart of the historic city, tearing down the seventeenth-century merchant houses of the Briggate. The University buildings became a railway station: its wide gardens were covered with marshalling yards.

This was a real sentence of death on the ancient High Street and all about it. If the rulers of the University had held their ground for a few years, we should probably have seen in Glasgow what Dublin has, a famous college with its garden giving character and clear air to the centre of the city. As a university quarter the reconstructed High Street would surely have found a respectable and thriving life again. One imagines the University expanding towards the new open space of Cathedral Square, an admirable setting for academic life. In fact, the rebuilt High Street, though decent enough, lost nearly every trace of its old activity and character. The City Improvement Trust, through which the

Town Council worked, approved some handsome buildings at Gorbals Cross and in the Saltmarket, but the face of Glasgow was turned permanently westwards and many of its people scarcely know the streets where its history grew.

The main framework of the city was now fixed. Renfield Street, Union Street, Jamaica Street, Bridge Street, Eglinton Street—a continuous highway, though so variously named—formed a sort of backbone from north to south across the modern Glasgow bridge, taking the central place that the High Street once held. Its proper culmination on the south (now cut off by cross-streams of traffic) was Queen's Park, on the hill of the Langside battle. This line was crossed from east to west by two others. One was Argyle Street, prolonging the ancient thoroughfare of the Trongate and Gallowgate. The other, high above the river flats, was Sauchiehall Street, carried east to the neighbourhood of the old Townhead by Parliamentary Road. The modern visitor who keeps this scheme of things in his head will find that the rest of Victorian (and modern) Glasgow can be tied into it fairly easily.

The railways, which did so much to destroy Glasgow's origins, transformed the city's life in ways that were, perhaps, even more fundamental. They ended its physical isolation. Edinburgh was not much more than an hour's journey away, and after 1849 it was possible to reach London in nine or ten hours. But the sense of remoteness did not disappear. One can feel it in the rhetoric of Alexander Smith's verse:

> The wild train thunders in the hills,
> He shrieks across the midnight rills,
> Streams through the shifting glare
> The roar and flap of foundry fires
> That shake with light the sleeping shires;
> And on the moorlands bare
> He sees afar the crown of light
> Hang o'er thee in the hollow night.

"Thee" is Glasgow, a city still at the end of the world.

Victorian Glasgow remained a remarkably self-sufficient place. It had established itself as a great industrial city before the

112

28   Royal Crescent, Sauchiehall Street
Alexander Taylor, architect

29   The Royal Exchange, now Stirling's Library
David Hamilton, architect
Both from James Pagan's "Sketch of the History of Glasgow", 1847

30　Moray Place, Strathbungo
Alexander Thomson, architect

31　Park Circus
Charles Wilson, architect

32　Royal Exchange Place: archway to Royal Bank Place
Archibald Elliott, architect

33 The "Park Towers" (Park Church and Trinity College) from Elderslie Street

34 Cathedral Square Church (1880) now Barony North
John Honeyman, architect

35 St. Andrews Hall (1873): West Front
James Sellars, architect

36 Free Church College (1856), now Trinity College
Charles Wilson, architect

37   Early Victorian lay-out: Park Terrace and Park Circus (*Charles Wilson, architect*) from the University Tower

38   Kelvinside Academy (1887)
James Sellars, architect

39   Great Western Terrace (1870)
Alexander Thomson, architect

railways came. It looked towards the sea, and steam had given it a new playground that could be reached without rails. It had the Firth of Clyde at its doors, with a great series of sheltered lochs running under the Highland hills. Steamers that sailed from the heart of the city had opened the way to those things before Victoria was Queen. Kirkman Finlay had retired to a romantic castle at Toward. All Glasgow did its best to follow him, if only for a week in July, and, a decade or more before the railways arrived, steam coaches helped to establish the "Famed Loch Eck Tour". For a generation or two, Glasgow on holiday scarcely wished to look further than the Cowal fiords and the Ayrshire beaches. The Highland shores of the Firth were soon covered with summer villas and cottages. It is entirely characteristic of the time that Alexander Thomson, whose mind was full of Greece and Egypt, should have spent almost all his holiday time in the Isle of Arran, should have visited London only once or twice in his life, should never (it seems) have reached the Continent at all. Business men might use the trains to London pretty freely, but to most Glasgow people it was as much a foreign city as New York. A Scot in London felt himself provincial only in the sense that a Bruxellois or Genevan might consider that he was meeting the great world in Paris.

The people of Victorian Glasgow formed a social pattern that was very much their own. Many a prospering business man would have recited "A man's a man for a' that" with true emotion and have claimed, with a good deal of truth, that no barrier of class could prevent an able young Glaswegian from rising as high in the city as talent and luck could take him. Yet classes existed, and the distinctions between them were strongly felt. A series of famous murder cases, still well-remembered and often discussed, though the first of them is nearly a century old, bring out the strength of this feeling in the crises of life and death.

Partly, at least, it was because she was the daughter of a highly respectable architect that the story of Madeleine Smith's illicit passion for a poor clerk from the Channel Islands shook her native city with such delicious horror. Perhaps it helped to win her the verdict of "Not Proven" at her trial in 1857, when he had died, rather too conveniently for herself, after drinking the cocoa she had given him. A working class wife, Jessie McLachlan, and (much later) a wandering Jew, Oscar Slater, were conspicuously less fortunate.

Meanwhile, the economic basis of Glasgow life was changing again. Cotton no longer dominated trade. It remained very important till the 'sixties, when the American Civil War, which cut off supplies of raw material, killed it almost as suddenly and dramatically as the American Revolution had destroyed the trade of the Tobacco Lords.

In this case, however, the break need not have been final. Lancashire went through a depression far greater than anything that the west of Scotland suffered at that time, but the cotton industry revived there quickly enough. The truth seems to be that Glasgow men had simply lost interest in the business which had made the place an industrial city. The foundry fires were far more exciting and profitable.

Glasgow sat among coalfields; indeed on them. Old and forgotten workings are often rediscovered in the most unexpected places; on the slopes about the University, for instance. The first ironwork was established in 1786. But the city's first great expansion was not based on coal, and it was not until 1830, or thereby, that the foundries became really important.

By that time manufacturers had learned to understand that their part of the world had been endowed with a peculiar wealth of its own—the blackband ironstone in which ore was mixed with coal. The invention of the hot blast by a Glasgow man, J. B. Neilson, made it possible to use this profitably. Almost at once the shires—North Lanarkshire and Ayrshire particularly—and the city itself glowed with foundry lights.

The Bairds of Gartsherrie were the typical figures of this development—five sons of a farmer who leased Lanarkshire mines, set up furnaces and were soon enormously prosperous. One of them particularly, James Baird, is a great figure in Glasgow legend. In his later years he gave half a million to an evangelistic foundation within the Church of Scotland. It is said that another eminent ironmaster once chaffed him on the subject.

"Man, for all the money you've given to the Kirk, I take ye a bet of five pounds that ye can't repeat the Lord's Prayer."

"The Lord's my Shepherd, I'll not want," replied James Baird, going rather slowly through the first verse of the 23rd Psalm in the metrical version.

"Man, I did not think you could have said it," exclaimed his challenger, producing a £5 note.

It is a characteristic Glasgow story, but the state of mind it suggests was not at all typical of Victorian Glasgow. Its rulers were still, in the main, educated men, and education was highly valued. One of its heroes was David Stowe, a cotton spinner, who, following Chalmer's lead, revised and reformed schooling for the working class and established a famous Normal School for the training of teachers.

Social life, indeed, was inclined to become more serious and home-keeping. The dancing assemblies of earlier days died away as the houses of prosperous people became large enough to allow them to hold balls at home. For most reasonably prosperous men, business was absorbing. The Scottish production of pig-iron swelled till, in the 'sixties, it was a third of Great Britain's. And it was at this stage that Clyde shipbuilding and engineering really rose towards supremacy. Local iron made iron ships, and in these the river could lead every other. It is not, after all, surprising that when the American War cut the supplies of raw cotton, its place in the city's business was easily taken by other things.

Mid-Victorian Glasgow was supremely self-confident. It seemed to have overcome its worst problems, or to be overcoming them —slums, social discontent, even a banking crisis of its own. For that reason a second bank failure hit it particularly hard. The end of the City of Glasgow Bank closes an epoch. Scottish banking had a remarkable history. In some respects it certainly led the world—above all in the trust which companies that had no backing from the State had earned for themselves. The City Bank was the youngest of the big Scottish institutions and had sometimes been thought to be the most enterprising. In 1878 it stopped payment. It was an unlimited company. Each of its shareholders was liable for its debts. Most of them were local people. The first call on them was for five times the amount of the investment. The majority found themselves ruined. Those whose fortunes survived paid up 2750 per cent. Depression swept over the wintry city. Factories closed, buildings stood half-completed. The directors were tried for fraud and imprisoned.

Nearly eighty years later, this catastrophe still echoes in Glasgow memories. For the first time, perhaps, it raised serious doubts about the future in the minds of Victorian Scots.

Cresce diu, felix arbor, semperque vireto!★
O utinam semper talia poma feras!

quoted one of them, a few years later, glancing at the tree in the Glasgow coat of arms. "The wish, unhappily, is vain. Glasgow has lived through many a trying season, and probably she has still vitality to revive now. But the *felix arbor* is not sound at the roots. Chicago and Glasgow have been likened to each other for their rapidity of growth. But Chicago depends on wheat, which grows, and Glasgow every year more and more depends on minerals, which do not grow. Here and there grass grown blocks of slag tell where a great iron-work once blazed, that has blazed its ironstone all away; or a weather-blown heap of shale tells where the panting engine has sent up its last hatch of coal. As the exhaustion of minerals advances, our industry, and with it our commerce, must fall back, and the general suffering can only end when the population shall have shrunk in keeping with the reduced power of production."†

★ Still grow and flourish, happy tree,
　　Forever strong and green !
　Oh that forever you may bear
　　Such fruits as we have seen !
† J. O. Mitchell in *Memoirs and Portraits of One Hundred Glasgow Men*, 1886.

CHAPTER SEVEN

Glasgow Flowers

1880 to 1914

AFTER all, the Happy Tree continued to grow green, and to bear its accustomed fruits as well. If Glasgow was, perhaps, a little less self-confident than before the City Bank crash, if the foundations of its wealth in ironstone and coal sometimes seemed a little less native and solid, it grew steadily richer. The output of ships, of machines, of the score of lesser industries that had fed its outward cargoes since the eighteenth century, continued to swell. Scottish iron was being changed into steel. From 42,000 tons in the year of the bank failure production rose to 1,000,000 in 1900.

The city swelled too. It absorbed the suburbs and dependent towns that had grown round it: only those which, like itself, had roots in the Middle Ages—Rutherglen, Paisley, Renfrew— resisted annexation and are still independent. It could not move fast enough to keep pace with some of its prosperous citizens: along the railway lines dormitory villages began to grow for the benefit of those who worked in town but wanted to live "in the country". But throughout the later Victorian years, and even after them, most wealthy Glasgow people had their homes in Glasgow. The great terraces of the first West End, which are now filled with business offices, clubs and consulates still housed merchants, manufacturers and professional people till the motor car arrived to take each of them individually to his own corner of a neighbouring shire.

The Tree of Glasgow now had conspicuous flowers as well as fruit. The first of them was leisure. It is true that there was no class, however prosperous, which was content to do nothing beyond enjoying life. But, at last, there was time to relax a little.

The prosperous man of early Victorian days had been so intensely busy that there was usually very little room in his life for anything beyond his business, his home and his church. Public affairs were controlled largely by men who had been able to win "an independence" when they were still young: like Robert Stewart they were apt to absorb themselves in the business of the Town Council or in organising churches and charities—or to retire to a new sort of life on country estates. The wage-earner had very little spare time, except on Sundays, when he was often willing enough to rest.

The late Victorian began to find that it was possible to work just a little less. He could begin to play. Golf, which had flourished on the Green before Glasgow's one public park was improved into a state of level featurelessness, had disappeared in the early Victorian years. It now revived again. The great days of football began. The Association game became the absorbing interest of Glasgow working men. At first it was played by amateurs who now had free Saturday afternoons for themselves, but the interested onlookers soon far outnumbered the players and, long before the end of the century, most of the leading clubs were professional. Rugby football, which in Scotland has remained strictly amateur, gave the middle class a similar sort of interest.

There was even time to think about the leisure of the young. The Boys' Brigade, founded by a young Glasgow man, William Smith, in 1883, seems to be the oldest of all the "youth movements" that now fill the world—a pattern for the Scouts to come, even (remotely) for Komsomol and Hitler Youth. The Brigade, however, remains true to its origins, which were markedly religious, though it has grown rather less military than it once was. In its native place it is still strong.

Music, too, began (or began again) with Victorian amateurs. Famous virtuosi had visited Glasgow from time to time, but the societies which organised regular concerts in the eighteenth century and later seem to have died away under the early Victorians. Music became, in the main, a thing for homes and churches. There were fierce battles over the first church organs.

The piano came into Glasgow homes, and the early nineteenth century sang Scots songs in its drawing-rooms. Then the new leisure produced choirs and amateur orchestras. Professional players were needed to support singers who were performing "the Messiah of Handel on a scale proportionate to the greatness of the work". Regular Saturday concerts drew musical Glasgow to the new St. Andrew's Hall, and, in 1893, the Scottish Orchestra was formed to provide symphonic music for the whole country, though it was still linked with the Glasgow Choral Union.

The growth of leisure interests touched painting, too, with results much more noticeable outside Scotland. Like other cities, early Victorian Glasgow had had its group of artists, mainly portrait painters. They even founded a West of Scotland Academy in 1840. Its annual exhibitions were revived by the Glasgow Institute of Fine Arts, which prospered and built itself a home in Sauchiehall Street. Its charmingly pure Greek façade, now part of a drapery store, was the first work of the future Sir John Burnet. No doubt these recurrent shows helped to develop a habit of patronage among prosperous people.

Such connoisseurship was not a new thing in the city, but it had been rather doubtfully regarded. There were ancestral memories of the sad fate of the Foulis Academy collection of masterpieces, many of which had been found to be wrongly ascribed and valueless. In the 'Forties, Bailie Archibald Mac-Lellan, a man of fine taste, had formed a great collection of his own. He built a handsome gallery for it in Sauchiehall Street, and when he died in 1854 he left both pictures and building to his town. The legacy was received with suspicion, all the stronger because it proved to be burdened with debt. It was suggested that many of the paintings were not genuine. Under this cloud some were sold very cheaply. With difficulty the Town Council were persuaded to pay £44,500 to secure its ownership of the building and pictures together. Then it was discovered that MacLellan's choice had, in fact, been remarkable—that the city had made a brilliant bargain. It was the real beginning of a municipal collection that is the finest of its kind in Britain.

No doubt this story did something to encourage later business men to take the risk of spending time and money on paintings. Glasgow art dealers and their customers soon showed themselves percipient and enterprising. They were not at all inclined to be overawed by the accepted fashions of the Royal Academies of London and Edinburgh.

"In Glasgow", wrote one of the leading spokesmen of the new artistic life that was to surprise the city, "there never was, nor at the present moment does there exist, either a controlling power vested in a body of artists, or an indication of opinion arising from a cultured lay community. Artists were, and still are, free to do what they like, provided always that they take the consequences of their own ways and works. The business man buys what he likes, or is persuaded to like, or because it pleases him; it would be hard to find a city where there are collections of pictures showing greater honesty of purpose".*

Among many other things, Glasgow connoisseurs of the late 'seventies and 'eighties bought the work of French Impressionists before it was much appreciated elsewhere in Britain. This was seen by local painters. By the middle 'eighties Glasgow had Impressionists of its own. They rejected the reigning academic ideals of high finish and almost photographic exactness. Their interest was in pattern and, above all, in colour. None of them was as great as the great Frenchmen, but to academic critics and painters they were revolutionary, and the best of their work is very good to look at still. When it was shown in London in 1890 it seemed sensational. When it was transferred to Munich it gave birth to artistic "secessions" from the academic standards of Bavaria and Austria.

It excited Glasgow, too—not only the local collectors, but the newspapers and their readers. No doubt European recognition of what was called "the Glasgow School" flattered the city. But, undoubtedly, the paintings themselves were found pleasing. When they were hung in the Institute shows, the town flocked to look at them. They appeared on the walls of restaurants and

* Francis H. Newbery—Introduction to The Glasgow School of Painting by David Martin (1897).

40 The City Chambers, George Square: built in the late 1880's
William Young, architect

41 Business palazzo in Gordon Street, now chief office of the Commercial Bank of Scotland
David Rhind, architect

42 "Egyptian Halls", Union Street
Alexander Thomson, architect

the new tea-rooms. People who had never shown any particular interest in art—who, perhaps, had scarcely known that such a thing existed—were soon discussing W. Y. Macgregor and Joseph Crawhall, John Lavery and James Guthrie, the Japanese journey of George Henry and E. A. Hornel.

It was a moment when Glasgow felt itself in touch with the world—in touch and on show as it had never been before. The second half of the century was the great age of exhibitions. Perhaps it was partly the wish to prove that it had recovered completely from its bank crash and the industrial depression of the mid-'eighties which made Glasgow put on an International Exhibition of its own in 1888. No doubt this had some serious industrial and commercial purpose: financially it was a notable success. But its white palaces and towers among the trees of Kelvingrove had far more important effects. They taught Glasgow people to enjoy themselves and look for amusement through a whole summer. They brought scores of thousands of strangers into the city, so that the railways cut an hour and a half off their running time from London and raced one another to establish new records.

The profits of the Exhibition were used to provide a new art gallery, itself surely designed to be part of a great fair, rather than the more serious spirit that usually shapes public buildings. It was ready for use on the day when a second exhibition opened, in 1901—then it housed what seems to have been a very remarkable show of painting. The experience was repeated in 1911. Thrice in thirty-three years, the great town of business, steel, and smoke turned itself into a pleasure city. The sun shone, orchestras played. Gondolas or (in 1911) motor boats flitted about the Kelvin—less fouled by the effluent of industry than it is now. The western sky, in the evening, was bright with reflected gaiety. The Second City of the Empire could feel itself (temporarily) to be the centre of the world.

The Glasgow that visitors to these exhibitions saw was changing, though the main structure of its modern shape was firmly fixed before the first of them opened. It had cut itself off from its river. For centuries its people had looked down from their bridge, or bridges, on its shipping—first the few lighters and fishing boats, then the forest of masts and funnels that lined the long quays. The first dock had been opened in 1867. Others soon followed. From these, or from the Tail of the Bank, off Greenock, the Glasgow liners—Anchor, Clan, Allan, City, Donaldson—sailed west or east. Beyond the docks stretched the shipyards. But unless they passed close to the river, or travelled on it in the little "water-buses" of the time, the Cluthas, the eyes of Glasgow people could seldom catch these things. A mass of girders, the bridge that carried trains into the new Central Station, concealed most of the active Clyde from them. It is only in the past generation that the George V Bridge has again opened the prospect of that astonishingly narrow stream which feeds the town. But if late Victorian Glasgow could not watch the Clyde it could hear it. The occasional horns of ships, the constant rattle of riveting echoed as far as its containing hills.

The spirit that welcomed exhibitions was breaking into the streets, to vary but not always to improve them. Well before the first of these shows, office buildings began to grow into Italian palazzi—a fine specimen by David Rhind, of Edinburgh, is the western block of the Commercial Bank in Gordon Street, but there are many more. Nearly all of them are well-executed and handsome, but much more imitative than earlier Victorian buildings. Two large shop buildings of cast-iron and glass (one as early as 1856)* do not break the style noticeably. Buchanan Street, already (and still) the first of Glasgow's shopping centres, must have had a pleasantly restful pattern when the latest things in it were Charles Wilson's Royal Bank façade and his block opposite the present Stock Exchange, while the vista was closed by David Hamilton's re-built St. Enoch Church, removed twenty years ago. It was first broken by things that were pleasing enough in themselves, such as James Sellars' Renaissance building for the *Glasgow Herald*, with the well-shaped high arches of the counting house behind it. Sellars was the foremost Glasgow architect of his generation. The western façade of his St. Andrews Hall, and his Kelvinside Academy are impressive pieces of classicism.

* At 36 Jamaica Street. The designer is unknown.

Sellars' successors in and about Buchanan Street were often ruthless enough in their disregard for the earlier scheme of things. It is possible to take a kindly view of their great, pinnacled buildings, often in the new red stone of the 'nineties and later. "Looking down West George Street on a summer's evening", says a writer whose taste cannot be questioned, "it seems to hold 'many-towered Camelot'* at its foot." No doubt there was something Tennysonian about the romanticism of the new office blocks: like Tennyson, they are not quite Gothic, but often glance in that direction. In autumn mists or the soft rain that gives pavements and streets the look of rivers, some of them loom and reflect themselves rather impressively. For half a century, more or less, they have been an essential part of the Glasgow scene. But in spirit they surely belong to the time of the exhibitions: in them the wealth and optimism of late Victorian and Edwardian Glasgow are permanently on show.

The great show building of municipal Glasgow was opened in the year of the first exhibition—the towering palace of council rooms and offices which is the City Chambers in George Square. Here, surely, the Corporation† had set itself to prove that Glasgow had fully recovered from the disaster of 1878. The sense of wealth in the place is too insistent. Designed by a London Scot, William Young, it breaks from its massive base into pillars and statues, balconies, vast colonnades and galleries. The interior is full of Italian marbles, alabaster, mahogany, and satinwood. Yet it is beginning to have a sort of period charm. The work of painters of the Glasgow School appears, rather oddly, but pleasantly enough, in the opulent banqueting hall. Above all, the cupolas echo across the Glasgow horizon a form first seen in Robert Adam's Trades House but repeated most effectively by late Victorian architects. "Glasgow of the steeples" was an old Gaelic phrase. There are plenty of steeples still, but the town has become a place of domes and round-headed towers.

The reaction to this rich profusion was maturing as the century

* In J. H. Muir's *Glasgow in 1901* (see p. 91).
† The Town Council now prefers to call itself the Corporation of the City of Glasgow.

ended. The name it bears is that of Charles Rennie Mackintosh, the most original of all the Glasgow architects and a pioneer of the modern functional style. Only a dozen years or so separate the beginnings of his School of Art from those of the City Chambers; yet the School can still shock traditionalists a little and excite other people by the freshness of its forms.

Mackintosh was wholly a Glasgow man. His father was a police superintendent. He got his training in a local architect's office and in the Glasgow School of Art. No doubt he learned something from the head of the firm he joined, John Honeyman, who had designed the cast-iron Ca'doro building and was also interested in an earlier tradition of Scottish architecture than the classical one.* What is called "the Scottish vernacular" was already attracting other architects like Sir Rowand Anderson (designer, in Glasgow, of the Central Station and the Pollokshaws Burgh Hall, a beautiful evocation of Scottish baroque) and Sir John James Burnet in his less classical work.

One side of Mackintosh's style no doubt grew out of this movement. It is possible to catch (or, at least, to imagine) a faint reminiscence of the old University building, transformed in a mind that was re-thinking everything for itself, in the lower, northern façade of the School of Art. From other aspects—the eastern one, especially—the towering walls suggest a medieval Scottish castle, just as the rough, white-washed stonework of some of the studio interiors recalls (surely quite deliberately) a Scottish barn, and there are iron grills that hint at portcullises. But the whole building is designed strictly (and very successfully) to meet the practical needs of an art school. The site, on the steep south slope of Garnethill, is difficult and restricted, so that this masterpiece, though it hangs just above the throngs of Sauchiehall Street, is not easily seen. There is scarcely a detail of the place, inside or out, that belongs to any convention which was established in 1896, or for long years after that. And yet everything is the architect's own doing. The Governors of the

* One of John Honeyman's most attractive buildings however, is completely and surprisingly Italian—the former United Presbyterian Church in Cathedral Square which is now called Barony North.

School wanted something cheap and simple. It is certainly simple, even stark, from some points of view, and was cheaper than anything else half as original could have been expected to be. At the beginning of this century there was nothing like it in the world. It is, says Dr. Howarth, "the synthesis of traditional craftsmanship and twentieth-century engineering", and "the first important architectural monument to the new movement in Europe."★ Though Mackintosh has influenced two generations of designers in many countries, there is nothing else really like it in Glasgow now.

When his design for the School of Art was accepted, Mackintosh was twenty-eight, a draughtsman in the office of John Honeyman and Keppie. Eighteen years later, he left Glasgow, but his effective work there had ended some time before that. It is sometimes suggested that he was unhonoured and unappreciated in his own town, but this is scarcely true. Opportunities came to him as early as they do to most men. His hand is clearly seen in the tall red sandstone water tower and façade at the back of the *Glasgow Herald* office in Mitchell Street (1893–4) though parts of the design and most of the decoration are evidently his employers'. He produced a church (Queen's Cross) and a remarkable school (Scotland Street, recently half-masked by a factory) besides a number of private houses. Naturally there was criticism and even ridicule of so original a talent. But his work became a part of Glasgow's life in places much more familiar to most people than the School of Art—the city's most admired tearooms.

The Glasgow of that time was intensely proud of these places. And with reason. One of the best and rarest books about the city, *Glasgow in 1901* by James Hamilton Muir (the pseudonym covers Muirhead Bone, James Bone, and A. H. Charteris) welcomes them as a new wonder of town life. It is pointed out that women who, in the past, had found it hard to meet and eat outside their homes, and men who had had very little choice between the pub and the club, used them equally.

★ *Charles Rennie Mackintosh and the Modern Movement*, by Thomas Howarth.

"It is believed (and averred) that in no other town can you see in a place of refreshment such ingenious and beautiful decorations in the style of new art as in Miss Cranston's shop in Buchanan Street. Indeed, so general in the city is this belief that it has now caused the Glasgow man of the better sort to coin a new adjective denoting the height of beauty; for in describing his impression of some uncompleted buildings at the Exhibition, he was heard to use this climax: 'It is so kind o' artistic, ye know, wi' a' that sort o' light paint. Oh, it'll do A1! It's quite Kate Cranston-ish'."

The "ingenious and beautiful decoration", or some of it, was Mackintosh's. Catherine Cranston, the daughter of a prosperous hotel-keeping family, was the chief creator of the new style of Glasgow tea-room, which helped to transform social habits. She was a famous and picturesque figure in the city. Mackintosh began to work for her in 1896, and was soon closely associated with her projects. His decorations and those of his wife, Margaret Macdonald, who was his partner in such designs, are beautiful and original enough. Perhaps they made even more of a stir in the world than his building. But they have a *fin de siècle* quality which dates them more sharply. For Miss Cranston he also designed furniture, cutlery, interiors and one entire tea-shop, "The Willows", whose decorative scheme was based on the name of the street where it stood—Sauchiehaugh, "the willow meadow". Part of its façade survives in Daly's Sauchiehall Street store. A glimpse of one other Mackintosh-Cranston creation can still be caught at Ingram Street behind a display of jewellery and shopfittings: it was rescued from destruction by Glasgow Corporation. Messrs. Daly, too, have preserved something of the "room de luxe" which was one of Edwardian Glasgow's glories. All the rest of the Mackintosh that Glasgow knew best is gone. Yet the city had welcomed and enjoyed him. He was greatly admired by modernists in Austria, Germany and France, though he made no impression on England even when he settled there.

It seems likely, indeed, that his genius had simply burned itself out in the ten years of intense activity when most of his work in Glasgow was done. One is tempted to imagine how he might have influenced Scottish building after the First World War if he had continued to hold his place at home—above all, if he had been able to train and inspire younger men. Then local councils were faced with the demand for vast new suburbs of small houses. Mackintosh had worked out a pattern of house-building (seen at Windyhill, Kilmacolm) which might conceivably have been adapted to this new need. The material to be dealt with, harled brick, was one that he could handle. As it was, very few of the new schemes had any real character or any reminiscence of Scottish traditions. When architects and designers of practical and adaptable genius were most needed, Mackintosh had lost heart and had left no successors.

Though the idea that the building of new houses anywhere outside the streets that had been cleared of slums should become a public service had scarcely dawned on late-Victorian town councillors—and was very unwelcome to most of them when it did appear—the men in the new City Chambers were busy enough. No doubt the theory of "milk and water socialism" stirred some of them, but Glasgow had begun to develop a whole series of new services before Fabian ideas on the subject were influential. The Corporation was as full of optimism and enterprise as its electors. To wait for the direction of Governments was not in the Victorian mood.

The success of their water scheme and their Health Department had set off the rulers of Glasgow on a new course. They took over the gas supply from private companies. The first general service of electricity was a municipal one, launched in 1893. They even developed municipal telephones—so successfully that, by 1907, there were more subscribers in Glasgow than in five of the largest English provincial cities added together, and rentals were far below what the Post Office could offer when it took over the city's exchanges.

Glasgow had had a system of horse buses since the 'forties and of horse tramways since 1870. In 1894 the Corporation took control and proceeded very quickly to electrify its trams. For a generation or two these brightly painted cars, swinging like ships through the streets, were a source of enormous satisfaction to

Glasgow people. They were clean, regular, and well-kept. The city built them for itself, and felt they were far, far better than the rattling vehicles which served other towns. In the new age of electricity, Glasgow was going ahead, not just as a centre for private enterprises but as a unit. If Socialist ideas grew and spread, this was partly because the old spirit that had made merchant Glasgow a sort of city republic had revived to give point to them.

Later Victorian, even Edwardian Glasgow was not, however, a Socialist city. It was, as it had been since the Reform Bill, mainly a Liberal or Radical one. And it discovered, surely with a sense that the political world was, rather belatedly, taking a proper turn, that it could be a breeding ground for Prime Ministers.

Its Liberal Premier came out of the drapery business. The Victorian town had begun to produce great stores—the proper Glasgow name for them is "warehouses"—whose wide façades helped to fill Sauchiehall Street, Buchanan Street and Argyle Street. Drapery warehouses in the more usual sense of the word were equally important: they supplied shopkeepers not only in the West of Scotland but wherever Glasgow ships sailed. One outstandingly successful firm which combined both types of business had been founded by two brothers, born MacOran, who, for reasons which apparently lay deep in family legend, changed this very distinctive name to Campbell when they came to the city.

The elder of them became Lord Provost and Sir James Campbell of Stracathro. Henry, his second son, was a man of high intelligence, as he proved at Cambridge, after passing through the High School and the University of Glasgow. He remained a draper, however, until he grew absorbed in politics. Mr. Campbell-Bannerman (he took the second name as the heir of a maternal uncle) became Liberal M.P. for Stirling Burghs, though his father was a strong Conservative. He was genial, sensible, sincere, a good party man—and a devoted follower of Gladstone. The House of Commons thought him admirable, and even Ireland liked him when he was in charge of its affairs. He could have been Speaker, but the party, shocked after its Home Rule crisis, needed him as a rallying point.

43   Scotland Street School (1904)
C. R. Mackintosh, architect

44   Wellington Church (1883), University Avenue
T. L. Watson, architect

45   The West Front

46   North Façade
in Renfrew Street

Amiable as he was, he could show the rock of principle where it was needed. When the aftermath of the Boer War brought down the Conservatives in 1905, Sir Henry Campbell-Bannerman was found to be the only possible Prime Minister. In Labour affairs and in South Africa, he was an effective peacemaker, and when his health broke down and he retired in 1908, he carried the respect of his colleagues, and of Glasgow, with him to the grave.

Three years later another Glasgow man became leader of the Opposition. Andrew Bonar Law had been a highly successful pig-iron merchant, the leading figure of the "Iron Ring" on the Glasgow Exchange. He, too, had been a High School boy, though he was born in Canada. His Premiership, when it came, was to be even shorter than Campbell-Bannerman's, but Glasgow expected it longer. In the last years of the century of peace, the rise of these politicians could strengthen and confirm the feeling that the city was no longer on the world's fringe but very near its centre. Yet it remained entirely itself and seemed more than ever its own master. Its last exhibition, successful as usual, had been a Scottish one—Glasgow people looked with pleasure on its reconstruction of traditional Scots buildings, and its profits founded a Chair of Scottish History in the University.

With the new century, building lost, by degrees, some of its late Victorian exuberance. Windows that had bulged for a generation began to flatten again. They were used, notably by John A. Campbell, to give vertical effects that are particularly striking in his Northern Assurance building in St. Vincent Street —unfortunately in Portland stone. This architect, who had been a fellow-student of John J. Burnet's at the Beaux Arts, designed a number of office blocks notable for their dignity and restraint. These were almost the last days of stone tenement building on the old scale, but the tradition was still alive and (apparently) developing. Here, too, the bow windows of the 'eighties and 'nineties were at last coming under control. A distinguished example of Edwardian tenement work—remarkably enough, in grey stone—can be seen at the corner of Shields Road and Ter-regles Avenue, within sight of Greek Thomson's Moray Place.

It was designed by H. E. Clifford, the architect of a number of Gothic churches remarkable for their well-proportioned simplicity.

Industry and trade were rising to new heights after a serious depression. All the fruits of the Victorian age were ripe. It was true that the Clyde yards were full of warships and that, for a year or two back, holiday-makers on the Firth had seen lines of great dreadnoughts steaming out of Lamlash Bay to target practice. But the German bands still played in the streets. The news from Sarajevo scarcely creased a forehead. And then, on 4th August, 1914, the age was suddenly over.

CHAPTER EIGHT

The University

THE University is so much a part of Glasgow's history that it has been impossible to keep it, or the names of its famous men, out of the earlier chapters of this book. Glasgow has never been a university town in the way that Oxford, Cambridge, and St. Andrews are. The University has never dominated the city. But it is not a sort of educational appendage, tacked onto a great town because there were plenty of potential students there, as most of the modern English universities and many American ones have been. Through most of its past, it has been an essential part of Glasgow's equipment. It has brought intelligence to the place and has taught its leaders to think. Many things in this book's story would have had a different shape and flavour, some very important ones could scarcely have happened at all, if the University had not been there to form their development.

It had an odd beginning. The first Scottish university, St. Andrews, was founded at a time when, politically, the Scots kingdom was at one of the weakest points in its history. Forty years later, when Glasgow University came into existence in 1451, things were not much better. The Crown was in the midst of a critical struggle with its most powerful subjects—a sort of shadow in Scotland of the fearful dynastic wars that tore fifteenth-century England, France, and Spain. It is a dramatic proof of the national vitality and self-confidence that, in this age of confusion, the Scots should have determined to provide their country with a kind of learning in search of which students had been forced to travel to Paris, Oxford, or Cologne.

It has been argued that the new University itself came out of the wars. Bishop William Turnbull, its founder, and Lord Hamilton, who gave it a home of its own, were both Douglas men who turned to the King's side in the contest between James II and the great house which might have displaced him. Turnbull seems to have been a man of high intelligence. He had studied at St. Andrews and Louvain and was a doctor of Pavia. He was the Pope's man as well as the King's. Nicholas V gave him the bull that authorised the establishment of the University, and King James backed him by freeing its members from taxation. But though it had privileges, teachers, officials, and students, it had no property and scarcely any endowments when Bishop Turnbull died. Its meetings were held in the Cathedral or the Black Friars' monastery in the High Street. Probably most of its original masters were themselves friars or cathedral clergy.

Bishop and King may have planned Glasgow University as a school of law and theology, but the Faculty of Arts was the only one that established itself securely. The first universities of the Middle Ages grew up in places where crowds of young men had flocked together to learn from famous masters. The universities themselves were self-governing guilds of masters—or sometimes of students. They chose their own officials, notably the rector who was their president. Usually there was also a degree-conferring chancellor, who was the local bishop or his deputy. Glasgow had officials of this kind from the first. But by Bishop Turnbull's time the average student arriving at a university was no longer a young man but a boy in his middle 'teens. Such students needed to be guided and disciplined. The old, almost republican, sort of university government did not work so well where they were concerned. What suited them was something more like a school, with a headmaster.

In Glasgow, they got such a head very soon. His name was Mr. Duncan Bunch. It is worth remembering because he was the forerunner of a long series of university principals—certainly of the Glasgow principals and, just possibly, of most principals, presidents and permanent vice-chancellors in other universities. Finding the new little foundation without a home of its own, the first Lord Hamilton decided to give it premises next to the

Black Friars' Monastery—buildings which it may, perhaps, have been hiring already. He called this creating a college, but he gave his site, with the land behind it, not to a college in the English sense—a small group of masters and students inside a university— or to the University itself but to Duncan Bunch, principal regent of the Faculty of Arts. The regents were the teaching masters, so that the principal regent was, in effect, the head teacher.

From that day in 1460 forward, the principal was the real, working head of the place. Glasgow had the beginnings of the sort of organisation which, in the eighteenth and nineteenth centuries became normal in new English-speaking universities on both sides of the Atlantic and many other parts of the world. It is possible to argue that this Glasgow set-up (which was more or less accidental) was copied first in Aberdeen, then in Dublin and Edinburgh, and finally in a hundred other places which had never heard of Duncan Bunch—that it was the first gift of Glasgow University to the world.

The University, which was henceforth mainly the College of Arts, developed rather slowly. It had one famous teacher, John Major, a great doctor of Paris, philosopher and historian— though Rabelais did not think much of him. Its greatest names are those of Robert Henryson, the poet, and David Beaton, the cardinal.* At the Reformation it almost passed out of existence, though Mary Queen of Scots came to its rescue with some endowments from the old Roman Church. Its principal was a Protestant and its influence seems to have strengthened the new faith. But it was not till 1574 that this could be fully felt. In that year, Glasgow College got the greatest principal in its history.

He was Andrew Melville, from a family of small lairds near Montrose who had welcomed the first stirrings of the Reformation. And he was one of the most learned scholars of Protestant Europe. He came home from Geneva in 1574 determined to educate his own people. St. Andrews wanted him, but very soon he was settled in Glasgow. At once he began to pour new learning into the college. Students who had heard of little beyond Latin

---

* A John Knox matriculated in 1521, but it is now believed that this was not the future reformer.

grammar and Aristotle (in Latin) now met Greek, the classical literatures, mathematics, geography, history, Hebrew and the other biblical languages, besides Calvin's theology. Melville was a brilliant and persuasive conversationalist, who passed on his knowledge and ideas to friends and colleagues as well as to pupils. He was also a man of colossal energy and endless courage. It was these qualities and the influence they gave him which finally established Presbyterianism as the national system of church government in Scotland.

They showed clearly enough in Glasgow. There were two students there who were closely related to Lord Boyd, the most powerful man in the city's affairs. One of them, Mark Alexander Boyd, was also nephew of the Archbishop. He was to write what was probably the finest Scots sonnet, but he was a rebel in every classroom. His friend, Alexander Cunningham, was a cousin of the Earl of Glencairn. Between them, the Boyds and Cunninghams controlled a large part of the country south and west of Glasgow.

Mark Alexander had been punished by his regent, James Melville, the Principal's nephew, and devoted chronicler. In revenge, the two boys waylaid James Melville and might have killed him. The Principal brought the affair before the Rector of the University and the Privy Council, and Alexander Cunningham, who had used a sword in the encounter, was ordered to beg forgiveness publicly.

On the day set for this ceremony, the Earl of Glencairn and Lord Boyd and most of the gentry of North Ayrshire, some hundreds of Boyds and Cunninghams, rode into Glasgow. It was the sort of demonstration that had often over-awed Scots law courts, and even Parliaments. The Principal's friends pleaded with him to forget the whole business. But he would not be moved. Before it was admitted, he said, "that we dar nocht correct our scholars for fear of bangsters and clanned gentlemen they sall haiff all the bluid of my body first!" With the Rector, the regents, and the body of red-gowned students behind him, Melville faced the men in arms outside the cathedral. Young Cunningham defiantly offered to make an apology, if any would accept. "Doŭbt nocht of the acceptatioun: we are heir readie", said the Principal. The thing was duly done, the "clanned gentlemen" went home peaceably, and the discipline of the college was re-established.

By this time Andrew Melville had won a new constitution from the formidable Regent Earl of Morton. This *Nova Erectio* was the framework of the University's affairs for nearly three centuries. It provided for a Rector, elected annually by masters and students, for a Dean of Faculty (the sole relic of the old Faculty of Arts) and for a Principal, three regents and four endowed scholars (bursars) who formed a college in the proper sense of the word. Some funds were assured. It was still a tiny foundation, but students who were prepared to pay for their learning flocked into Glasgow. There was, James Melville proudly claims, no place in Europe comparable to it "for a plentifull and guid chepe mercat of all kynds of langages, artes and sciences".

That was a comprehensive boast. When Andrew Melville left Glasgow for St. Andrews after six years it was, of course, impossible to find an equally distinguished and energetic successor. But the life he had given to the college did not disappear. It flourished modestly and its influence on the whole life of the west of Scotland grew deeper as it sent out its annual freshet of thoroughly taught ministers and educated laymen. It probably did more than anything else to make Glasgow itself an intensely Protestant and Presbyterian city.

There were some distinguished names among Melville's successors: Robert Boyd of Trochrig, a gentle but strong-principled theologian who loved music; John Cameron, the wonder of schools, who reconciled predestination and free will, went into exile, and was killed in the streets of Montauban; John Strang, "the learnedest Covenanter in Scotland"; Robert Baillie, whose letters help us to understand what the Covenant Wars meant to an intelligent and sensitive Scotsman; Patrick Gillespie, an ambitious academic politician and friend of Cromwell.

The College was rebuilt, mainly by Principal Strang's efforts, though the work was completed in Gillespie's day—as fine a specimen of Scottish baroque as could be found anywhere, before it was turned into a railway station and finally taken to pieces. It filled a good part of the eastern side of the High Street, where the College Goods Station and its warehouses are now. There were two courts—later three—and the rebuilt Blackfriars Kirk next door was a sort of college chapel. Behind the buildings, a great garden stretched east across the Molendinar. To begin with the regents and many of the students lived in college, but in the eighteenth century, as more room was needed for a bigger teaching faculty, the students tended to move into the town and the professors (the name "regent" had disappeared) were given houses in a new court on the north. What was really important was that they were in the centre of the city, a minute's walk from the Cross. The burgesses were conscious of the College and it was equally conscious of their affairs. The sons of merchants regularly finished their education in the classrooms, though few who were not going into professions (the church, particularly) may have taken degrees. Professors and townsmen were continually meeting and talking. While many academies concerned themselves only with the classics, pure mathematics and theology, Glasgow early began to develop an interest in economics and experimental science.

In a sense, the middle and late eighteenth century saw the College's greatest days. Perhaps it is fair to say that a good deal of what made the Golden Age of academic and literary Edinburgh had its beginnings in Glasgow. William Cullen, in medicine, and Joseph Black, in chemistry, taught in the High Street before they moved away to found schools in the capital. The Glasgow school of philosophy, which began with one of the last regents, Gershom Carmichael, spread its influence through Frances Hutcheson and Adam Smith.★ It affected David Hume, who wished, in vain, to succeed Smith as Professor of Logic, and its last great name in the eighteenth century was that of his ablest critic, the enormously respected Professor Thomas Reid.

The learned and convivial, but notoriously absent-minded Robert Simson, Professor of Mathematics, was a sort of social

★ See Chapter IV.

president of that society, who would meet him in rural Anderston of a Saturday, for a dish of hen-broth and an afternoon's conversation. "He used to roll a lemon or orange in his hand when he was working out his problems and the lost propositions of Apollonius Pergius," wrote one of his pupils, who became Earl of Buchan. "Some College Waggs once scaled his chamber window and, insinuating themselves unobserved, stole away the orange or lemon and replaced it with a Turnip. When the problem came out well solved, out came the Professor with his Eureka. In the College area he met with Foulis the Printer.

" 'Robin,' said he, 'man, what's that in my hand?'

" 'Ou dear Professor,' said Robin, 'what makes ye ask me? Why, it's a Neep.'

" ' A Turnip, you blockhead, that's impossible, for it was an orange when I was busy and I never had a Turnip in my room in my life.' "★

It seems that the problem of this metamorphosis was gravely discussed, perhaps even solved, at the next meeting of the Professor's Friday Club.

But the really explosive personality of the college was John Anderson's. The blast of his memory still raises echoes after the best part of two centuries. He was a student at Glasgow, then Professor of Oriental Languages (this, oddly enough, was apt to be a stepping stone to other chairs), then for thirty-nine years (1757–96) Professor of Natural Philosophy. He does not seem to have contributed a great deal to the theory of physical science, though he was an intelligent and inquiring man and one of the professors most apt to meet distinguished strangers—notably Dr. Samuel Johnson on his rather disastrous visit to Glasgow. He was, however, a stimulating and successful lecturer, deeply impressed by the comparatively new idea of teaching through experiment. He was one of those who befriended and helped James Watt. And he quarrelled most comprehensively with the majority of his colleagues.

The difficulties of Glasgow University's curious constitution were now beginning to appear. Nearly all the property belonged

★ Quoted in *Memoirs of the Old College of Glasgow*, by David Murray.

to the College. The Principal and the professors who formed its governing body now called themselves "the Faculty". But there was also a University council, headed by the Rector. This Senate was composed of much the same people, but disputes were constantly developing between the two bodies. John Anderson made himself a sort of leader of the opposition to the. Principal. He was almost constantly at law with the official majority. On many points he seems to have been right, but this, naturally enough, did not endear him to the other side. His classes grew. He had developed a special evening course which men who were not regular students were encouraged to attend, and, since he took a keen interest in new industrial processes, this attracted and helped to train manufacturers and craftsmen. But, though he had many admirers in the city and a core of good friends in the College itself, he became, more and more evidently, a sort of formidable and cheerful odd man out.

Then, in 1796, the real explosion came. John Anderson died, and it was found that he had left behind him a plan for creating a rival university in Glasgow.

It was not much more than a plan, an idea. A painted chest containing "money, jewels, gold, silver, medals, bonds and bills" was to go to his relatives. The whole of his other property was given "to the Public for the good of Mankind and the Improvement of Science, in an Institution to be Denominated 'Anderson's University'". But this large legacy was found to consist of apparatus and a little museum, worth altogether about £1,000. These could not be sold. As an endowment for his proposed university of four "Colleges" (i.e. faculties) and thirty-six professors they were not too impressive.

But he had also left his idea, and his friends. Anderson was attempting the impossible, and, as so often in Glasgow's history, the impossible was almost achieved. Successive writers who may be said to have been in a sort of apostolic succession to his colleagues in the High Street have dismissed him as a ludicrous buffoon, "Jolly Jack Phosphorus", and his plan as a joke. But it has produced one of the most remarkable and flourishing institutions in Glasgow, the Royal Technical College. Anderson's

University did, in fact, become what was perhaps the first technical college in the world. It was the model for the Royal Institution and Birkbeck College in London (named after its second Professor of Natural Philosophy) and for countless Mechanics' Institutes elsewhere in England. It also produced, in Glasgow, a College of Medicine which had many famous teachers and was only extinguished (surely regrettably) in 1947. All this grew without endowments or grants of the modern kind because the scheme of an institution which could be attended by all who were willing to learn (including women) was so attractive, and, essentially, so practical. Anderson's friends were prepared to work for his idea and manage the "university" that he had failed to endow.

To-day the Royal Technical College★ is probably the largest school of technology in Britain outside London, and certainly one of the most effective. One clause of Anderson's will, which declared that "no person connected with the University or College of Glasgow" must have any part in his institution has certainly not been carried out, for the two bodies are affiliated. But the idea of an independent technical university is still alive, and events may be carrying his foundation in this direction.

John Anderson had been one of the professors who were rash enough to cast a friendly eye on the beginnings of the French Revolution. No doubt this did not endear him to some of his colleagues, but it was not until the very end of the long war with France that political suspicion raised a real stir in the College. A later liberal, James Mylne, Professor of Moral Philosophy, acted as chaplain, and on the Sunday after the news of Napoleon's escape from Elba reached Glasgow, he was unlucky enough to begin his service with the 107th Psalm:

> When straits them press
> They cry unto the Lord, and He
> Them frees from their distress—

★ The Glasgow and West of Scotland Technical College was founded in 1886 by a fusion of institutions, but the chief of them, Anderson's College and the College of Science and Arts, had developed from the original Andersonian University. It became the Royal Technical College, Glasgow, in 1912.

and to end it with the 26th Scottish Paraphrase:

> Behold he comes! your leader comes
> With might and honour crowned!

Some hearer decided that this was sedition: the congregation had been induced to prepare itself spiritually for a Napoleonic invasion. The Sheriff of Lanarkshire made a searching inquiry. No other trace of Bonapartist conspiracy could, it seems, be found in the unlucky Professor's speech or conduct. The University's loyalty was duly, though a little grudgingly, acknowledged. There is no reason to think that it has been questioned since 1815.

The great light of the nineteenth century, the professor whose name meant most in the town of Glasgow (and outside it) was William Thomson, Lord Kelvin.* His father was Professor of Mathematics, and William Thomson himself entered the University in 1840. Apart from five years at Cambridge, he was to remain a member till 1907, when he died Chancellor.

His age, when he matriculated, was ten and a half. The thought will shock modern educationists: though students no older than schoolboys were common enough, the future peer was years below the average, monstrously out of alignment according to present-day theories. What is still more shocking by these standards, he proceeded to carry off prizes in nearly every class he entered. The first of these (for Latin) were won before he was eleven. At the age of twenty-two, already a fellow of Peterhouse, Cambridge, he became Professor of Natural Philosophy.

Probably it is still impossible to value or judge his work properly. Its range was enormous and he was so little self-assertive and so ready to pass on ideas to others that research is needed to establish his contribution to the vast advance of nineteenth-century discovery and invention. He was once asked to write a series of popular articles on the mariner's compass. The first appeared, but five years passed before the second was

---

* The title under which he was best remembered was taken from the river which flows through Kelvingrove Park, below the modern University. He received his peerage in 1892.

47   The Old College, High Street
From Pagan's "History of Glasgow", 1847

48   The Old Merchants House and Steeple, Bridgegate
(Sir William Bruce, architect)
From a lithograph by William Simpson in Stuart's "Views and Notices of Glasgow in Former Times" (1848)

49   The University (*Sir George Gilbert Scott, architect*), from Kelvingrove Park

written. In the meantime he had changed his subject: having turned his mind to the compass, Thomson had developed and improved it till it had become almost a new instrument. The principle of the famous Second Law of Thermodynamics was first stated by him. But he worked almost equally effectively on contrasting branches of physics. His mind was alive to the technical developments around him and it fed Glasgow industry with new ideas.

In his day, however, the University was transformed, and in a way that tended to take it out of the intimate life of the city. Both materially and in law, the old College vanished. In 1858, an Act of Parliament abolished the Faculty and the remains of *Nova Erectio*. A new body, containing some members who were not professors, the University Court, took control of finance and property. The graduates were given a General Council—a revival, but not a very effective one, of the medieval Congregation. Specialist faculties were organised. Medicine and Law had made a beginning in the eighteenth century, but their development had been held up by the predominance of old privileged corporations, the Faculty of Physicians and Surgeons and the Faculty of Procurators, which gave professional training. The University's Medical School now established itself firmly, but though, under Kelvin, Glasgow's scientific prestige was very high, a separate Faculty of Science was not created till 1893, and the Faculty of Engineering appeared thirty years later.

As the number of professorships swelled, the Senate (which still looks after teaching and discipline) became, perhaps, a little unwieldy. The Rector, whose office was now honorary, was elected by the students only—they usually chose a politician. It was a new world, but one which can leave the Principal (successor to Mr. Duncan Bunch) perhaps more powerful than ever.

Meanwhile the professors (and very notably the professors' wives) were growing unhappy about their old home. The other side of the High Street had become a slum, and they were not prepared to wait for the day (actually not far ahead of them) when its ancient houses would be cleared and rebuilt.

"In Glasgow", wrote Lord Cockburn, who had been Rector,

"the voices of the few men of sense, who are in horror, are drowned by the howls of the selfish mob that is impatient for the sacrifice. The Professors expect to gain chiefly by getting better houses, and even they are insensible to the value of age to an academic retreat. Yet [the Old College] is one of the most academical edifices in Scotland, and all the better for being in the heart of a crowded population. This deepens its contrast. The very silence of either of the two quadrangles when a person (with a soul) turns into them from the roaring street, inspires thought and study.

"There is a grey stone image, something like a leopard, perched on one of the pillars of the great outer stair leading up to the hall. It has sat with its fore-legs up and its pleased countenance, smiling graciously on many generations of teachers, students and strangers. The head of this single creature is more worth preserving than the heads of all the professors."*

In Cockburn's day the old building had a reprieve, because the University's effort to sell it to a railway company broke down. But in 1870 it was deserted for a new home in what was then the extreme West End of the city. Its site, on the southern ridge of Gilmorehill, is certainly a wonderful one. The University looks out across Kelvingrove Park to the Clyde, the shipyards, and the uplands beyond the river valley. Its spire can be seen from half the hilltops within 20 miles. The building is one of the few important ones that Glasgow has taken from a London architect (Sir George Gilbert Scott, of the Albert Memorial) and almost the only secular thing of any size which imitates Gothic. It cannot be said to be very successful: its rectangular length and central tower suggest a nineteenth-century mill, with chimney. It can be impressive at night as it leans over the dimly lighted gate that leads past Sir John Burnet's friendly Union building† to the professors' quadrangle.

And some things from the old College have been preserved. The lion (for it is not a leopard) with its attendant unicorn once more look out from the old stairway. Part of the old façade from

---

* *Journals of Henry Cockburn*—entry for 28th November, 1845.
† Originally the Men's Union, this is now occupied by women students.

the High Street, now twisted into a rectangle and mounted on stilts, serves as a gate lodge, and is still worth looking at. But though the city has grown round it and the high streets of Hillhead make a pleasant university quarter, the new building has never become a part of the town as the old one was. More than half of Glasgow is hardly aware of it, and perhaps there are times when part of the University is only half aware of Glasgow.

The buildings which, in 1870, seemed enormous are now merely the core of an expanding institution which has been both spreading into new corners and (one way or another) annexing what were recently independent colleges. Perhaps it is too big and complicated to have quite the personality of its past, or to bring out professorial personalities in the same way. Perhaps this is the age of the team rather than the individual. But it can be said that in this century the students seem to have overshadowed their masters, at any rate in the eyes of most Glasgow people.

Since 1870 there have been many principals and professors famous and influential in their day—nearly every Glasgow graduate must owe a debt to one or more of them. Their greatest achievement was to keep student minds lively. Student generations pass quickly and usually are soon forgotten except by their own members and their teachers. But one, which flourished in the years before the first German War, has left a legend. Its most famous leaders were Walter Elliot (now a Right Honourable elder statesman) and O. H. Mavor, who was to be James Bridie. They and their friends filled the *Glasgow University Magazine* (now generally known as *GUM*) with some of the best light verse any publication of the kind has ever seen. They found a new student anthem. They enlarged the spirit of comradeship and discussion. Half a century later a good many of them, perhaps, remain students at heart.

Theirs were the last days of a student race almost exclusively masculine. Women had appeared at Gilmorehill, but they were few. A Glasgow Association for the Higher Education of Women, which wished to provide teaching on a university standard, had been formed in 1877. It was backed by a remarkable Principal, John Caird, who was also a supporter of the Glasgow painters.

In 1883 it established a college, which took its name, surprisingly enough, not from Queen Victoria, but from St. Margaret of Scotland, the mother of King David who re-established the Glasgow bishopric. Queen Margaret College settled itself a mile or so from the University in North Park House, which is now the Glasgow Headquarters of the B.B.C. Nine years later it became part of the University, and its students were able to take degrees, but till 1914 most women continued to be taught there. Now "Q.M." survives only in the name of the women students' union.

The city which may not always be conscious of its professors, certainly sees the students when they come into its streets, queerly dressed but cheerful, in the January cold and mist of their annual Charities Day. It reads about them or watches them, often with a disapproving (but, perhaps, fundamentally indulgent) eye, when they hold the triennial battle of the rectorial election, or receive the chosen Rector with howls and paper missiles. And it may sometimes have the feeling that, in our day, it has been the students rather than their professors who have provided it with ideas. Three times they have surprised and interested Glasgow by their votes for Scottish Nationalism. Twice Nationalist Rectors* have had something to say to them that was, at least, a good deal less obvious and expected than the contents of most political addresses of the older sort.

Time is needed no doubt to discover the men whose work is going to seem most important for the future. But it will be strange if Glasgow University, students or teachers or both, fails to influence twentieth-century Glasgow as it has influenced and often guided the Glasgow of other centuries.

* Sir Compton Mackenzie (1931-4), and John McCormick (1950-3).

CHAPTER NINE

Forty Years and the Future

TO look at, Glasgow has changed very little in a half-century that has shaken the world. It is bigger, though its population now grows slowly. Miles of little houses—and, now, of new high tenements, more impressively described as "multi-storey flats"—fill the floor of the Clyde valley from the line of the Roman Wall under the Kilpatrick Hills, to the braes of Renfrewshire. To some Glasgow people, this expansion seems enormous and inexplicable: they can scarcely believe, what is true enough, that, in the main, it has been caused simply by the movement of citizens from crowded flats, where tens of thousands of families lived in one room apiece, to the Corporation's suburban cottages. On the outskirts you can no longer step out of stone-built streets into the open fields. But the centre of Glasgow is still far closer to the country than the main streets of most great cities are. A dozen miles or so out you can be at the top of a 1,000-foot hill pass, with nothing in sight but heather. In summer you can board a steamer under the shadow of the great railway bridge that will take you, past the towering cranes of the shipyards, to the hills of Argyll.

To a returned Edwardian, even a late Victorian, there would be little that was surprising in the central streets themselves. Here and there a great building of the nineteen-twenties or nineteen-thirties perpetuates the classical tradition—the head office of the Union Bank (now united with the Bank of Scotland) is a good example. Here and there are twentieth century creations which even the age that created them would willingly let die. Cinema frontages break the lines of masonry. The longest and best known of the shopping places, Sauchiehall Street, still has

the oddly incomplete look it has carried for the best part of a
century. But elsewhere the cliffs of stone offices, terraces and
tenements sweep across the hillsides and open great canyons into
the valleys. The cupolas and towers hang in the sky. Though
dulled by smoke except where the western rains have swept it,
the Victorian city stands almost as solidly and handsomely as ever.

The bombing war scarcely scarred Glasgow, but in the last
half-century it has survived something that its people found
worse than war, nearly twenty years of depression. In 1914 the
recruiting offices were besieged. Glasgow's contribution to the
voluntary armies of the First German War was remarkable. There
were battalions of clerks and business men, students, tramway-
men, even under-sized "bantams". The losses, particularly at
Loos, were concentrated and shocking. The Clyde industries—
shipbuilding, steel-making, engineering—were of a kind on which
war made the heaviest possible demands. But there was also in
the city a Radical tradition of pacifism, which certainly had something to do with a famous clash between Glasgow trade unionists
and the Government, when the socialist *Forward* (brilliantly
edited by a future Cabinet Minister, Tom Johnston) was sup-
pressed for reporting a meeting at which Lloyd George's persuasive oratory failed to sway discontented workers. Several Labour
spokesmen were later exiled—to Edinburgh.

This had something to do with the emergence into politics of
what was called "the Red Clyde". A brief slump that came
immediately after the war's end produced strikes and the only
moment of violence that modern Glasgow remembers. It was
portentously named "Black Friday", but was not, by any
historic standard, a very serious business. On the last day of
January, 1919, crowds gathered outside the City Chambers to
hear the Lord Provost announce that the Glasgow men (Bonar
Law and Sir Robert Horne) who were Prime Minister and
Minister of Labour respectively refused to intervene in their
dispute. There was a clash with the police, a good many people
were injured and some arrested including (the now Right Hon.)
Emmanuel Shinwell. But the depression passed away for a year
or two. War losses meant that there were plenty of new ships

to be built. And before the slump had properly settled down again, Glasgow had sent a new force into Parliament.

It was a sudden glory. In the House of Commons that went into the war Glasgow had one Labour member, who later joined Lloyd George's War Cabinet. After the 1922 election it had ten. In a sense, the Labour Party had come out of the west of Scotland. Its first leader was Keir Hardie, miners' organiser and Scottish Home Ruler. The Radical working class had convinced itself that the system of public services which had done so well in one city could transform the world: and, in the first place, Scotland. The new men from the Clyde were convinced Socialists. They went to Westminster determined to impose their *mystique* on their party. They backed a fellow-Scot for the Labour leadership, Ramsay MacDonald. Their electors felt certain that politics would be renewed.

But there was to be no new Glasgow Premier, at any rate in their day. Instead Glasgow found that, in Southern eyes, it had become a political and social Problem. Its needs, though not much noticed elsewhere till the arrival of the Clyde Socialists alarmed Westminster, were serious enough, especially in housing. The building of new tenements in the traditional style by private landlords had been checked just before the war, partly (though certainly quite unintentionally) by the Liberal Government's policies. After 1918 it could not begin again; the cost of such work was too high. And, meanwhile, the condition of existing houses was steadily growing worse. Rent control left the owners nothing that could be spent on improvements and very little for repairs, for in Scotland, though not in England, the landlords had to pay rates, which shot upwards yearly as the local councils were forced to find more and more money for the relief of the unemployed. Inevitably the slums, which had shrunk under the late Victorian improvements, spread wider and grew fouler again.

The Corporation and its officials struggled against the blight. Houses unfit for habitation were officially "condemned"—but thousands continued to live in them since, in a city still expanding (though slowly) there was nowhere else for them to go. Over-crowded or badly kept homes were "ticketed" and rigorously inspected. But conditions of life were often barbarously bad. The rest of Britain learned about them from an eloquent pamphlet by the late William Bolitho, "Cancer of Empire".*

"We enter the Close", he wrote, describing a visit to a single-room home in a "backland". "On each landing opens the water-closet, which the municipality installed thirty years ago. This is clean—the municipal inspectors are vigilant; but on an average twenty-five persons share its use. In some houses this number is nearer fifty. On the other side of the tiny landing opens a long, impenetrably black gulf; the central corridor of five homes. We feel our way, knock at a door and enter, calling out "Sanitary". A small room, one side of which is taken up by the Scots' fire-place, like an enclosed iron altar, with two hobs on which the teapot is kept everlastingly on the boil. The floor is worn wood, there are irregular square inches of frayed oilcloth. An enormous drabbled woman, who is dressed in dish clothes which do not show the dirt so plainly, however, as her face, explains the arrangements. . . . She has five children, and the gas is kept burning all day at the glimmer. The elements are simple and human. There is the bed, set into a niche, deep, evil-smelling, strewed with heaps of the same material as her dress. . . . Bed, hearth, and chair; humanity's minimum, as simple as the Par-ables. Under the window is the 'jaw box', the boarded, greasy sink, with polished brass syphon tap. . . . On the mantel-piece are two china dogs, and between them curious shapes of solid brass, which I take up and find to be rough profiles of women's boots, cut and scored out of a plate of metal. These or similar shapes of ships, money-boxes, pillar-boxes, are universal in Glasgow in the poorest den. So Art, and the making of things only for the eye, has left traces of itself even here."

Throughout the years of depression the Glasgow Councillors worked, not unsuccessfully, to replace the slums with new cottage suburbs, using all the Government grants they could collect for the purpose. For in Scotland the depression closed and deepened. A good many businesses slipped out of Scots hands, beginning with the railways and some of the banks. Glasgow had

* G. P. Putnam's, Sons, 1924.

50   Sunlight in the City: Waterloo Street

51   The River in the heart of Glasgow: the Broomielaw

52   The narrow Clyde and the Govan shipyards

built more railway engines than any other town in Britain, perhaps in the world. Amalgamation cut down the work in the shops of what had been its own railways and left the great North British Locomotive Company to depend almost wholly on foreign orders. One of the oldest west of Scotland industries, calico printing, disappeared altogether. The firms that carried it on were bought into a great English combine and their works shut down. Most of the Clyde's great shipping lines disappeared. The twenties saw one loss of this sort after another. Even steel and shipbuilding lagged.

For the first time Glasgow men failed to find new trades as the older ones dwindled. Attempts to break into the automobile and aircraft markets collapsed. While the English Midlands boomed, there was constant unemployment in the city. When the Great Slump of the early 'thirties swept over the world, something like a third of Glasgow's population was on the dole.

Even in the worst of the depressed years, the Happy Tree was putting out a flower or two. Twentieth-century Glasgow has at least the beginnings of a literary life of its own and has been creating a theatre. It has always been a city of readers: perhaps it is surprising that, on the whole, its memorable writers have been so few.

Tobias Smollett learned medicine in Glasgow. We get glimpses of its eighteenth-century society in *Roderick Random* and *Humphrey Clinker*—unflattering in the first book, kindlier in the later one. But the best of all Glasgow novels is still John Galt's *The Entail* (1822) which gives a vivid picture of the merchant who insisted on turning himself into a laird. The one Glasgow poet who made a resounding name for himself in the world (and in his own city) was Thomas Campbell (1777–1844)—it is doubtful if many, in this age, have glanced at *The Pleasures of Hope*. There was a good deal of writing in pre-Victorian and early Victorian Glasgow— the breezy violence of *Tom Cringle's Log* by Michael Scott still finds readers, and there were poets like William Motherwell, William Miller (who wrote "Wee Willie Winkie"), Alexander Smith and (later) David Grey and Robert Buchanan. A newspaper, the *Glasgow Citizen*, under Dr. James Hedderwick, gave some of these men encouragement. But Victorian Glasgow has left no novel that gives a really lively account of its life and people. The best thing of that sort did not appear till our own day: it is Guy McCrone's *Wax Fruit*.

The most widely read of all Glasgow books was a very little one, J. J. Bell's *Wee Macgreegor*. Its sketches of a small boy and his family were funny, and they were true. It swept the city in 1902 when its chapters appeared in the *Evening Times*. It captured London and the United States. Oxford held "Wee Macgreegor" tea parties, where it was read aloud—the dialect, in that southern accent, must have been something to listen to. It is still the most convincing (and most entirely good-humoured) picture of Glasgow working-class family life, just as Bell's reminiscences *I Remember* are the best record of the Victorian middle class.

Edwardian Glasgow was sketched skilfully enough by Frederick Niven (1878–1944) in books like *The Staff at Simsons* and by Anna Buchan (1877–1948) in *The Setons*. But Neil Munro (1864–1930) was the typical novelist of the years of Glasgow's artistic flowering. The work that he himself took seriously was historical romance, the latest fruit of the tradition of Walter Scott and R. L. Stevenson—the only kind of Scottish prose writing which the Edwardians expected to find impressive. There is an intense nostalgia in his stories of Argyll which gives life to books like *Gillian the Dreamer* and *John Splended*. But Munro was also a brilliant journalist: his paper, the *Evening News*, was for years the best expression of Glasgow intelligence. The Clyde stories of a Gaelic skipper that he wrote for it under the pseudonym of High Foulis are as lively as *Wee Macgreegor* and more varied. It will be a long time before Glasgow forgets *Para Handy*.

Munro left no real successor in either of the styles that were his own. But modern Glasgow has, what Victorian Glasgow never had, a group of competent novelists, among them George Blake (*The Shipbuilders*), Nancy Brysson Morrison (*The Winnowing Years*) and Roy Jenkins (*Happy for the Child*). In the depths of its depression it produced the first notable playwright in the city's history. James Bridie (1888–1951) was essentially a Glasgow man, amazed and charmed and troubled by the world about him;

deeply romantic, but continually laughing at his own romantic feelings. He was bred a doctor—but the time offered him a chance in the theatre, which was his natural home.

In a sense the stage had scarcely acclimatised itself properly in Glasgow before his day. It is true that successive Theatres Royal —in Queen Street, in Dunlop Street, in Hope Street—had been firmly established since the beginning of the nineteenth century and most of the great English players from Mrs. Siddons' time onwards had come to them. Some of the actor-managers were well-known figures in the town, and they had faithful and interested audiences. Before the cinema developed, there were more theatres in Glasgow than there are now.

But the stage remained, on the whole, something imported and external. There was a great popular public for opera. The first triumphant display of gas-lighting in 1818 was arranged for a performance of *Don Giovanni*. More than a century later it could be assumed that even if the stalls were thin for an operatic performance, the gallery would be full. But the only really native things on Glasgow stages were the dramatic versions of Walter Scott's novels—which drew crowds for a century—and pantomime. For a time most of the Glasgow actors whose names were widely known were "comics". The principal boy might be brought from London, but, in our century at least, a pantomime where all the humour was English and which did not have at least one scene full of kilts and Scots songs was not likely to get very far. On the other hand, successful Glasgow pantomimes can count on running not for a week or two at Christmas, but for months. For some reason, Glasgow sees itself in this particular sort of inconsequent fantasy which was at its height in the nineteen-thirties. Scots comedians flourished in the music hall, but, so far, as Glasgow was concerned, the crowning glory of W. F. Frame, Neil Kenyon, Harry Lauder, Tommy Lorne (the peculiar joy of the years between the wars), Will Fyffe, and Harry Gordon was their appearance in pantomime.

With all this, it was not till 1909, or thereby, that many Glasgow men began to think about the serious theatre as they thought about painting, books and music—as something, that is

to say, which could belong to the city. It was then that an ingenious, enthusiastic Englishman, Alfred Wareing, introduced the
first repertory theatre. Those were the great days of intellectual
repertory in England and Ireland. The Wareing company had the
support not only of able Glasgow men but also of Bernard Shaw,
J. M. Barrie (the one famous Scottish name among playwrights)
Arnold Bennett and John Galsworthy. The national triumphs of
the Dublin Abbey Theatre were beginning, but though the
venture called itself the Scottish Repertory Company it did
not attempt to imitate the Abbey: there was no particular
effort to train up Scottish players or find new Scottish plays.
In fact, the theatre did produce a number of very able
Scots actors and actresses. More important, on the little
Sauchiehall Street stage of what was then the Royalty and is
now the Lyric, Glasgow saw plays such as had seldom reached
it, plays that asked to be discussed, sometimes the first per-
formances of pieces that would be internationally known. The
company was increasingly successful, but in 1914 the war closed
it down.

The "Rep." and what was known about the Abbey had
roused a new ambition for a national theatre. No professional
company could be got together after 1918, but a very talented
band of amateurs set themselves up as the Scottish National
Players. Their policy was to look for Scottish playwrights. They
found some, of varying competence. Most important, they drew
in young Dr. Osborne Mavor, who wrote for them first as Mary
Henderson and then as James Bridie. Though most of his plays
were first produced in other places, Glasgow recognised its spirit,
sometimes its past, in the most notable of them—*A Sleeping
Clergyman, Mr. Bolfry, The Forrigan Reel, Dr. Angelus*. A second
body, the Curtain Theatre, showed a special interest in plays
with Scots dialogue. Its chief discovery was Robert MacLellan,
whose *Jamie the Saxt* is both the best play in the Scots tongue and
the most telling dramatisation of Scots history. During the
Second World War, Bridie and other enthusiasts established a
professional company, the Citizens.

All this, no doubt, was part of the general movement of

literary revival that is called "the Scottish Renaissance": it is the part that is peculiarly Glasgow's, though Scots drama has also established itself in Edinburgh, Perth and other towns and has captured a considerable place in the B.B.C.'s Scottish programmes. The Citizens' career has been various and sometimes uncertain, but the effect of James Bridie's talent, so peculiarly native, has probably fixed its future. It will be surprising if this new thing, the Glasgow and Scottish drama, does not maintain itself for a long time to come.

There was a trough in painting as the members of the Glasgow School died or were dispersed. For a while, it became insistently academic, but here, too, there are some signs of a revival, partly under the influence of the only survivor of the greater age, J. D. Fergusson. The memory of the 'nineties has helped to bring in a wonderful wealth of art. Sir William Burrell, once a Clyde shipowner, has given the city one of the most remarkable of all collections of Impressionist paintings and medieval and Chinese treasures. This will not be fully displayed until Glasgow finds itself a satisfactory gallery outside its own smoke belt, but parts of it are often to be seen. Bequests have brought notable prints and paintings to the University too.

Meanwhile in the working life of the city a new idea had begun to make itself felt—an idea new, at least, to industrial Glasgow. It was the national idea. Glasgow had always been Scottish enough, but in their businesses the Victorians had scarcely been conscious of their Scottish-ness—mainly, no doubt, because the control of Scottish industries, finance and materials remained in Scots hands without any concerted effort on their part. When, in the years of depression, the demand for Scottish Home Rule began to grow strong, many industrialists put their names to a resounding declaration which condemned it.

But a campaign for a Scottish Development Council, pushed most consistently by the Nationalist journalist William Power, gradually made headway. A long effort to diversify Scottish industry began. Its most effective and persistent leader has been the son of a Lord Provost, a Glasgow man educated in Glasgow, now Lord Bilsland of Kinrara, K.T. He has planted industrial estates and has headed the enlarged Scottish Council (Development and Industry). New light industries have been brought in to balance the native heavy ones.* The whole process has been planned with or through Government agencies of different kinds. It is something quite unlike what Glasgow has seen in the past: it seems certain that without the pressure of the Scottish national idea it could scarcely have been kept going. No one can reasonably doubt, nowadays, that the future of Glasgow depends on the future of Scotland in the twentieth century, just as it did in the fourteenth.

Before Hitler's War the beginnings of the new movement (and, of course, rearmament too) produced some recovery, but unemployment was still evident enough for many months after the struggle began. It has not reappeared since 1945. During the war Glasgow was busy enough and the Clyde was filled with ships which found it the safest port of entry to besieged Britain.

Some war-time hopes have been disappointed. The gallant struggle, led by D. F. McIntyre, to establish a Scottish aircraft industry and Scottish air services that would repeat the triumphs of Victorian Glasgow's shipbuilding and shipping was checked by the policy of nationalisation and is still in the balance. The native voice of the city is not so clearly heard as it once was. Of seven daily papers published in Glasgow, only the veteran *Glasgow Herald* and its partners *The Bulletin* and the *Evening Times* are owned in Scotland. But, one way or another, a good many new industries have been brought in. American firms have set up factories, following the example of two—the Singer Sewing Machine Company, and the engineers Babcock and Wilcox—which have been established near Glasgow since mid-Victorian times. The city has seemed to be settling itself not ineffectively into a new mould where politics and planning are almost as important as the older sort of individual enterprises.

The will to survive and succeed is quite as essential now as it was in the past. One veteran of the hopeful days of Clydeside

* In his indispensable book, *The Second City*, C. A. Oakley is at pains to show how varied Glasgow's industries remained even when the "heavies" were strongest. But during the inter-war slump, many light industries were lost, at least temporarily.

Labour—the only one of those eager Scots M.P.s who might, perhaps have been a Socialist Prime Minister if his interest had not been concentrated in his own country—has done a good deal to supply these things. During the Second World War, Tom Johnston, who had been the most effective Glasgow Labour propagandist, became a truly national Secretary of State for Scotland. Since then he has headed (successively or simultaneously) the North of Scotland Hydro-Electric Board, the Scottish Tourist Board, the Forestry Commission, the B.B.C.'s Scottish National Council. He is a type of the sort of national-minded Scot on whom Glasgow must now depend.

In the middle of this century Glasgow seems to hang in the balance. There are the makings of a sort of city just as great as anything in the past, but different from the eighteenth century merchant town or the centre of nineteenth century industry. It must be a place of industry and trade, but it has the chance to gather a certain established magnificence and civilisation. History has given it a great deal: tradition, good reason for civic pride, a shape and buildings that are fine enough in themselves but can grow finer, like those of many other stone-built cities, if what is really worth having is properly cared for, and the less satisfactory things are intelligently weeded away. For this sort of thing, however, for the proper enjoyment of what it has to offer itself and the world, an informed and deeply interested public opinion is needed. For more than two centuries Glasgow has been moving so fast that it has scarcely had time to look at itself. This period of growth is perhaps ending. The great Victorian city can now begin consciously to build up its own character, as it has consciously and deliberately swept away the worst of its old slums.

One would like to think that, in these last years, Glasgow has been gathering strength to be itself. There are plenty of influences abroad in the world that could destroy it: not only those which threaten an utterly devastating sort of war but subtler ones which tend to make it lean not on its own courage and self-confidence, but on other people. Yet if one thing in its past is clear, it is that the greatness and growth of the place have depended, first

167

and last, on the will of Glasgow men. Historical accidents have helped, or sometimes hindered, but without the solid determination of its people, their willingness to attempt what others must have thought unnatural or even impossible things, a great town could never have been created at this particular spot, where there was neither unusual natural wealth nor an inevitable gathering of trade routes, nor even a concentration of political power to draw men together. Without Wishart and Jocelin, the bishops who held up the Scottish kingdom, Glasgow could scarcely have begun to grow. Without the merchants who made it a centre of world trade before it had a harbour and the manufacturers who built its first great industry on native skill and foreign cotton the city of a million could never have existed.

It may need as much concentrated will, national as well as local, to keep the Happy Tree flourishing as have been needed to make it burgeon. When one sees the crumbling of the Greek Thomson churches, and of many more ordinary buildings which we do not know how to replace with anything like the same effect, when one watches stone painted as if it were London stucco, as well as when one thinks of more fundamental things—the acceptance, for example, of conditions under which very little can be done without the rulings (and the revenues) of a distant authority —one may be tempted to doubt the future. But Glasgow's pride in itself certainly exists and has deep roots. The spirit of national revival exists too. With intelligence, these things can make the city, hung between two worlds, a place that all the world will wish to know. It is a good sign, surely, that Glasgow should have been talking of plans to put itself on show again. But if new exhibitions or civic fairs are to be fully effective, Glasgow men must understand more clearly than they have sometimes done what it is in their inheritance that can mean most to other people, and to themselves.

SOME BOOKS ABOUT GLASGOW

BELL, J. J., *I Remember*, 1932.

BROGAN, COLM, *The Glasgow Story*, 1952.

CANT, R. G., and LINDSAY, IAN G., *Old Glasgow*, 1947.

CHALMERS, P. MACGREGOR, *The Cathedral Church of Glasgow*, 1914.

COUTTS, JAMES, *A History of the University of Glasgow*, 1909.

EYRE-TODD, GEORGE and RENWICK, ROBERT, *History of Glasgow*, (3 vols.) 1921–1934.

Glasghu Facies, comprising every history hitherto published, ed. J. F. S. Gordon, 1872.

HOWARTH, THOMAS, *Charles Rennie Mackintosh and the Modern Movement*, 1953.

JOCELIN OF FURNESS, *Life of St. Kentigern*, with *Anonymous fragment*, (ed. Forbes in *Historians of Scotland: 1874*).

KIRKWOOD, DAVID, *My Life of Revolt*, 1935.

MACGEORGE, ANDREW, *Old Glasgow*, from the Roman Occupation to the eighteenth century. 1880.

MACKENZIE, J. L., *Glasgow: a Short Account of Municipal Undertakings*, 1938.

MACKENZIE, PETER, *Reminiscences of Glasgow*.

MACKENZIE, W. MACKAY, *The Scottish Burghs*, 1949.

MACKIE, J. D., *The University of Glasgow, 1451–1951*, 1954.

MALLOCH, D. M., *The Book of Glasgow Anecdote*, 1912.

MITCHELL, J. O., *Old Glasgow Essays*, 1905.

MUIR, JAMES, *John Anderson and the College He Founded*, 1950.

MUNRO, NEIL, *The Brave Days*, 1931.

MURRAY, DAVID, *Memories of the Old College of Glasgow*, 1927.

MURRAY, DAVID, *Early Burgh Organisation in Scotland—Glasgow*, 1924.

OAKLEY, CHARLES A., *The Second City*, 1946.

PAGAN, JAMES, *Sketch of the History of Glasgow*, 1847.

POWER, WILLIAM, *The Face of Glasgow*, 1936.

PRIMROSE, JAMES, *Medieval Glasgow*, 1913.

SENEX (ROBERT REID), *Glasgow Past and Present*, 1884.

SHIELDS, JOHN, *Clyde Built*, 1949.

STRANG, JOHN, *Glasgow and Its Clubs*.

Some Glasgow Buildings

CHAPTER SIX

By Charles Wilson:
Park Circus   about   1854
Park Terrace   about   1854
Free Church College (now Trinity College)   1856
Faculty of Procurators' Hall   1854
Alexander's School, Duke Street (John Burnet,
   sen.)   1858
Park Church (J. T. Rochead)   1858
Bank of Scotland, George Square (J. T. Roc-
   head)   1869
By Alexander Thomson:
Holmwood, Cathcart   1855
Hutchesontown   and   Caledonia   Road
   Church   1855–57
St. Vincent Street Church   1857–59
Egyptian Halls, Union Street   1860
Moray Place   1862
Great Western Terrace   1870
By James Sellars:
St. Andrew's Hall   1873
Glasgow Herald Building, Buchanan Street   1875
New Club   1878
Kelvinside Academy   1887
Cast-iron warehouse, now Ca'doro Restaurant
   (John Honeyman)   1872
Cathedral Square Church, now Barony North
   (John Honeyman)   1880

CHAPTER SEVEN

Wellington Church, University Avenue (T. L.
   Watson)   1883
By Sir John J. Burnet:
Fine Art Institute, now part of Pettigrew and
   Stephens' store   1878
Glasgow Athenæum   1886–93
Barony Church   1886–1900
Savings Bank of Glasgow, Glassford Street   1900
Elder Library, Govan   1901–2

By C. R. Mackintosh:

Glasgow Herald Building, Mitchell Street (with John Keppie)	1893
Queen's Cross Church (St. Cuthbert's)	1898
School of Art	1897–1907
Scotland Street School	1904
Tea-room interiors, corner Ingram Street and Miller Street	1907
Northern Assurance Building (John A. Campbell	1909
Office block, West George Street and Hope Street (John A. Campbell)	1905
Tenement, Shields Road and Terregles Avenue (H. E. Clifford)	1908
Orchardhill Church, Giffnock (H. E. Clifford)	1913

INDEX

The numerals in **heavy type** refer to the *figure numbers* of the illustrations.